Memorials of St. Paul's School

Anonymous

BIBLIOLIFE

Copyright © BiblioLife, LLC

This book represents a historical reproduction of a work originally published before 1923 that is part of a unique project which provides opportunities for readers, educators and researchers by bringing hard-to-find original publications back into print at reasonable prices. Because this and other works are culturally important, we have made them available as part of our commitment to protecting, preserving and promoting the world's literature. These books are in the "public domain" and were digitized and made available in cooperation with libraries, archives, and open source initiatives around the world dedicated to this important mission.

We believe that when we undertake the difficult task of re-creating these works as attractive, readable and affordable books, we further the goal of sharing these works with a global audience, and preserving a vanishing wealth of human knowledge.

Many historical books were originally published in small fonts, which can make them very difficult to read. Accordingly, in order to improve the reading experience of these books, we have created "enlarged print" versions of our books. Because of font size variation in the original books, some of these may not technically qualify as "large print" books, as that term is generally defined; however, we believe these versions provide an overall improved reading experience for many.

MEMORIALS OF ST. PAUL'S SCHOOL

I. THE FOUNDING

II. SUBSEQUENT HISTORY

NEW YORK
D. APPLETON AND COMPANY
1891

TO

THE OLD BOYS OF ST. PAUL'S SCHOOL

THESE MEMORIALS

ARE AFFECTIONATELY INSCRIBED.

I. THE FOUNDING.

BY GEORGE C. SHATTUCK, M.D.

I.

I HAVE been asked to give some account of why and how I was led to try to do something toward the establishment of a boarding-school for boys in connection with the Episcopal Church. I had been a member of a public grammar school of the city of Boston, and at the age of nine I was sent to the Latin School, and was a member of that school for three years. Thence I went to the Round Hill School, Northampton, a principal reason for the change being the advantage of a country life. The school had been established nearly two years, and already had a great reputation; I was the seventieth boy and found there companions from all parts of the country. The effort to improve education was made there under favorable auspices. There were academies, at one of which Mr. Cogswell, principal of Round Hill, had been educated, where the instruction in Latin, Greek, and mathematics was very thorough. The boys boarded in private houses and went to the school to study and recite. But Mr. Cogswell's object was not merely to train the intellectual faculties and to supply the mind with knowledge. He wished to train the physical and moral faculties, and in order to do this he must live with the boys and have them constantly under observation and care.

Extracts from the prospectus of the school, dated June 20, 1823, from letters written by himself soon after its establishment, and from a pupil, written after the lapse of several years, will show what Mr. Cogswell proposed doing and what he accomplished.

"The promise which we give to parents is that we will be zealous in our endeavors to preserve the health and improve the morals and the mental powers of their sons. We must, on receiving the charge of them, be to them as parents.

"And hence the methods of discipline and government must be parental. There is a difference between severity and strictness. The one may be gained by the frequent use of punishments, while the other is best secured by gentleness and example. The relation of the pupil and tutor is that of the weak to the strong, of him who needs instruction and defence to him who is able to impart them. Keeping this principle in mind, we shall endeavor to govern by persuasion and persevering kindness. These will be sufficient for all who are neither perverse nor disinclined to study; for others the institution is not designed, and obstinate disobedience on the part of the pupil must ever be a reason for his dismissal.

"To read, to write, and to speak English with correctness, and, if possible, with elegance, are the first and most necessary objects of instruction. . . . An acquaintance with English literature must be commenced with the first efforts at learning to read and write the English language. The pupils must be encouraged to grow familiar with our great masters of prose and verse; and, however much attention may be claimed by other studies, we must always bear in mind that nothing can supply the want of a thorough knowledge of our own tongue.

"The study of the Greek and Latin classics is the next in the order of importance. They form the basis of learning and taste, both for their antiquity and their intrinsic excellence; and while the history of literature is made clear and the connection between the culture of ancient and modern times is explained by the study of them, the mind is well exercised and grows accustomed to fix itself on foreign and distant objects, the best foundation for philological research and the scientific knowledge of grammar is laid, and the acquiring of the modern languages facilitated beyond expression.

"Yet there is a distinction between the two languages when we consider them as forming a part of a useful education. No one science can be thoroughly learned without an acquaintance with the Latin tongue, while there is no science for the study of which the Greek is indispensably requisite. . . . A knowledge of the Latin tongue is, therefore, essential to a practical education, and no circumstances in the situation of our country can deprive it of its importance, its interest, and, we might add, its absolute necessity.

"On the other hand, the Greek literature surpasses the Latin in variety, interest, originality, and actual merit As those of the Grecians who in the first days of their culture excelled in tragedy, epic poetry, and philosophy had no predecessors to imitate, so they have never been equalled in succeeding times; and while among modern nations each contends that its own literature is the best, each yields the second place of honor to the Grecians. . . . While, therefore, all our pupils must learn Latin, we submit to the decision of parents whether their children shall be instructed in Greek. We shall aim rather to assist a few in learning it well than to excite a larger number to learn it imperfectly.

"We regard the study of languages as the proper basis of education, both because it provides the mind with the most salutary employment and exercises the powers of invention and judgment no less than those of comparison and memory, and because it furnishes the keys of knowledge for future use."

The first letter is dated October 12, 1823:

"Our number is twenty-five, of which fifteen are with us altogether, and ten day scholars from the village. We rise at six and meet soon after for prayers, study till eight, at which hour we breakfast, then play till nine; from nine till twelve study, dine at half-past twelve, play till two; from two to five study, sup at half-past five, play till seven, and then assemble for the evening occupation, which thus far has been reading only, as there was scarce one among the number who could read English decently. A little before nine they are dismissed and go to bed."

The second letter is dated October 26, 1823:

"I am very happy in being able to say that every day gives us the satisfaction of perceiving that we are not laboring in vain. In regard to order, correctness of deportment, and docility of disposition, we have made a progress with our pupils very far beyond my expectations—so much so that I really feel that the three last weeks of my life have been productive of more good to my kind than all the rest of it.

"For the last fortnight we have had a regular trial of skill in running round our wood, which is a measured distance of half a mile. Five minutes before eight we let the boys out for their morning exercise and head them in a race. We are all in perfect health and so contented on our little hill that we never go down. The boys have never asked to go off the hill on any occasion, although there have been military musters and cattle shows. We have no refractory boys, and in no case has any disregard or disobedience of our commands been shown. Still our task is a most arduous one, for although our children are docile, they are wild as young colts and require to be constantly curbed and guided by a very tight rein.

"We take a great deal of exercise—running, jumping, leaping, climbing, etc. Neither cold nor rain nor snow keeps them indoors at hours assigned for play."

To these statements we may add extracts from an account of the school given in his later life by one educated there:

"While the school owed much to the proved scholarship and genius of Mr. Bancroft, the historian, and to the large staff of officers under him, all 'Round-Hillers,' as they love to call themselves, agree in attributing to the singular combination of admirable qualities in the character of Mr. Cogswell its prosperity and success. He was a man who united as is rarely met the qualities of the man of study and of action. His head, filled as it was with the learning of America and Europe, could not overbalance his generous large-heartedness. So completely, without attempting it in any manner but by the direct display of his own character, did he win the respect and confidence of all his many scholars, . . . not war, not distance, not time, could ever break the bond which bound them to each other; and the clasp which held them all was their reverence and affection for Mr. Cogswell. . . .

"But the side influences of Round Hill were, perhaps, the best part of it, and are certainly what the scholars love and remember longest. Many another school has come up to as good a mark of training in its curriculum; many, no doubt, have been superior in the severities of classic study to Round Hill. Though one of the most distinguished Greek scholars of Germany and one of the most distinguished Latin scholars of America were at the head of the Greek and Latin departments, we can allow this; but let any one visit the lovely site of this school and he can readily imagine how many converging influences from such scenery acted upon these boys. . . .

"Mr. Cogswell's was an educational and training establishment which rendered the services of book-learning and study but accessories to the larger intention of making the man and the gentleman. He was in his school, as in one of his summer excursion walks, where he led off the procession, a boy of a larger growth and maturer experience, but nevertheless one of the party, and by no means a Jupiter Tonans frowning from his arm-chair on a raised platform aloof and apart from the rest. Indeed, his relation to the boys was scarcely even that of a teacher. He was the organizer, manager, and father of the community, while his partner, Mr. Bancroft, did a great deal more of the teaching; and a large staff of German, French, and Italians, as well as eminent young men fresh from our college training, all worked assiduously under his general supervision. His department especially was that of moral and affectionate influence, besides which he was head farmer, builder, gardener, and treasurer of the place."

The opening and successful carrying on of Round Hill School was in the writer's mind an epoch in the education of this country. The establishment of Dr. Muhlenberg's school, at College Point, was another epoch. In these schools distinct religious training was introduced and made a positive feature of the work.

Mr. Cogswell in his prospectus says:

"As the fear of God is the most sacred principle of action, there is none which should be developed with more care. Each day will begin and end with devotional exercises. The Lord's day must be sacredly observed, and the exercises of public worship constantly attended."

When the writer was in search of a school for his own children he did not find any in New England where he was disposed to put them. He had a country home in a healthy and beautiful spot, and as his boys must go away from home to school, he thought it well to try to start a school there. One cause for the Round Hill School being closed at the end of ten years was that it was strictly a private enterprise started by two very accomplished gentlemen, but with narrow means; and though later an act of incorporation was obtained and several gentlemen took shares, which were afterward surrendered, the fees from the pupils were insufficient to carry it on as it was commenced. The situation was admirable, in a beautiful healthy country with hills and a large river and a fertile valley, and near a town, the residence of people of culture and refinement. There was a large corps of teachers, and accomplished men from Germany, France, Italy, and Spain were among them. The modern languages were taught by natives. Mr. Cogswell and Mr. Bancroft had enjoyed advantages of education in this country and abroad, and were familiar with the schools and colleges of Germany and France, and the ideas and modes of education of those countries. Attention was paid to physical culture, and the first gymnasium in this country was there established. The writer had spent weeks at the College of St. James, and was intimate with the rector and teachers, and also with the Bishop of Maryland, who was mainly instrumental in establishing the College of St. James. Insufficient endowment was a principal cause of the closing of that college.

From such sources the writer derived his ideas of a boarding school for boys. The intellect can be trained and the mind furnished at a day school. Physical and moral culture can best be carried on where boys live with and are constantly under the supervision of the teachers, and in the country. The English public schools of renown, such as Eton, Rugby, Harrow, Winchester, and others, with their extensive play-grounds, show the advantages of such a situation. Outdoor exercise is thus secured. Green fields and trees, streams and ponds, beautiful scenery, flowers, and minerals, are educators. The things which are seen are very valuable, and may be used to teach of Him who made them, and thus of the things unseen. Religious teaching and training for beings such as we are is all important. The things of this world are engrossing; but boys ought to be trained not only for this life, but so as to enter into and enjoy eternal and unseen realities. The life of this world is short and uncertain. To live well here in the fear and love of God and with love to our fellow-men is not easy, and teachers and instructors who have learned and practiced the arts of so living and passing through this world as not to lose the things eternal are essential to the success of a boarding school for boys.

Land and buildings having been provided for beginning such a school as the writer wished to see established, the selection of trustees was the next step. The bishop of the diocese, the rector of St. Paul's Church, Concord, the judge of the United States District Court in New Hampshire, the Secretary of State, and afterward Governor of New Hampshire, the Chief Justice of Vermont, a judge from Connecticut, where successful Church schools had been established, four gentlemen from Boston, eminent in different walks of life, zealous Churchmen and interested in education, consented to serve as trustees, and took a warm interest in the enterprise. The most important step was the choice of a rector. The trustees had land and buildings, but no endowment; seven or eight boys were ready to enter the school. The enterprise was regarded as difficult, nor was it easy to find one capable of managing a work where a large growth should come from a small beginning. The trustees made a wise choice. The rector-elect had been trained at St. Paul's, College Point, and at St. James's, Maryland, and came from missionary work in a difficult post, where success had crowned his labors. He was told, You have possession of land and buildings, but we can not promise you a salary, and you must derive your support from the fees of the scholars. He began the work under these conditions. It was emphatically a work of faith. The rector had a helpmeet full of interest in the new field of labor, and with faculties and qualifications admirably adapted to it. They labored together for many years, success crowned their efforts, and at last the faithful, devoted, and accomplished wife was taken to her rest. We live in a democracy, but no one can read the life of the general of the army of the Revolution and of the first President of the republic without being impressed with the fact that the one man was essential first to the independence of the country, and then to the establishment of the new government. And for a school to be well managed with many boys and many masters, the rector must know how to govern himself in order to direct and secure the harmonious co-operation of the many teachers and many boys, and he must have full power and liberty, and the support and co-operation of the trustees. And here I would refer again to the history of Round Hill School and introduce a letter from a distinguished alumnus vouching for the important work done by the principal, how successful he had been in securing the affection and admiration of his pupils, looking back upon his influence after a lapse of thirty years.

J. Lothrop Motley to J. G. Cogswell.

VIENNA, *April* 26, 1865.

MY DEAR MR. COGSWELL: A short time ago I received a note from Mr. Wales, together with a little pamphlet which he was so thoughtful as to send me, knowing instinctively how much pleasure it would give me.

The pamphlet consisted simply of the remarks made by yourself at the testimonial dinner given to you at the Parker House by Round Hill scholars.

My first emotion was one of deep regret that it had not been my good fortune to be associated with so many of my ancient comrades in this affectionate tribute to one so venerated and beloved, and by none of them more so than by myself.

I read your beautiful speech with an almost painful interest; and, as I read it, forty years seemed to roll off my back and I was a small boy again in the never-forgotten chestnut groves of Round Hill. The tenderness and truth of the sentiments and the fidelity of the painting gave me a most sincere though melancholy pleasure much akin to that caused by the photograph of yourself which embellishes the first page, and in which I recognized at the first glance the familiar face of the benignant teacher and master of my childhood and the kind and ever-sympathizing friend of riper years.

It wouldn't be agreeable either to my taste or my feelings to make fine phrases about that beautiful little volume of seven pages which now lies before me as if it were the author's presentation copy of a new work; but I can't help saying that I have read it many times, and that the oftener I read it the more deeply do I feel that "simple truth is highest skill."

It produces on my imagination the effect of an exquisite idyl—exactly the effect which the greatest artist in words, if writing from the brain and not from the heart, would probably have failed to produce. I will say no more except to repeat my regret that I could not have been among the old pupils who paid this tribute not only to yourself, but to those three eminent and honored associates of yours, who, as I see, were also present at the dinner.

No, my dear old friend, not one of your numerous family ever thinks of Round Hill and of Dotheboys Hall at the same time except through the association of contrast, and I don't know how you could more adroitly have complimented yourself than by that protest. . . .

And with the most sincere prayers for your health and happiness I remain, my dear Mr. Cogswell,

Your ever affectionate pupil,
J. LOTHROP MOTLEY.

Certainly we may regard this testimony as to how much depends on the rector or head master of a boarding school and his power of winning the confidence, respect, and affection of the pupils as not out of place.

For a school must be large, attracting pupils from all parts of a large country, with various dispositions, talents, and requirements, many of them lacking the wholesome stimulus of prospective want. To mould such into a harmonious community, to inspire it with sentiments of truth, honor, and loyalty to God and man, is no slight task, and success in it can only be expected from one who has learned and practiced daily to bring his own body into subjection and to subordinate his own interest and preferences to a higher power.

St. Paul's School as it is now is the growth of thirty-five years, and yet much is to be done. An endowment, so that many boys whose parents struggle with narrow means can be educated there, is essential to the permanent success of a school the principal but not the only object of which is to educate the sons of wealthy inhabitants of large cities. These must be furnished with lodging, food, and with suitable comforts and elegances; and the furniture and equipments must be such as to gratify the taste and promote the refinement of those destined to take a prominent part in their after-life in various communities.

The celebrated English public schools were supplied with land, buildings, and an endowment sufficient for the maintenance of seventy or a hundred boys at the very start. There was provision to receive a much larger number on the payment of fees; and thus a very large number of active, useful, and distinguished men have been fitted for their life's work. St. Paul's began with buildings and land enough for a few boys only; year after year new buildings have been put up, adjoining land has been secured, and many boys whose parents could not afford to pay the fees of the school have been educated at a large reduction or gratuitously. The success from the small beginning has been most gratifying, but very much is still to be done.

A sufficient endowment, new buildings to replace the old, embellishment of grounds, completing the beautiful chapel, are objects still to be attained. New schools are springing up in all directions and with the same avowed objects; but the originators of these new schools do not, perhaps, sufficiently realize how much it costs to establish thoroughly and permanently a large school with an adequate endowment. We recognize how many have taken part and contributed to the advancement of St. Paul's School. No one of the first board of trustees is now a member of the board, and but one survives. The trustees now forming the corporation are a body worthy of respect and have important duties, and their character and repute attract to the school and inspire confidence. They have been very successful in the investment and care of the property. How much has been done by the present treasurer in a work extending through many years! Two of the present trustees are alumni, and assuredly it is a wise policy to look first to them in filling vacancies in the board. All friends of the school must recognize how much the alumni have contributed to its prosperity; and as we look backward to what has been accomplished and forward to carrying on the present work and furnishing necessary facilities for its extension, we may well thank God for his gracious strength and guidance in times past, and be instant in supplication for the wisdom and the strength necessary for success in the time to come.

GEORGE CHEYNE SHATTUCK.

II. SUBSEQUENT HISTORY.

Dr. Shattuck's account of the influences and circumstances which led him to found a School will be highly valued by all Concordians,* as well as by many other friends of St. Paul's.

It has seemed proper to append to the venerable founder's brief and modest statement a fuller narrative of what he has done, in order to show not only the extent of his benefactions, but also how far the purposes he had in view have been accomplished. At the same time the occasion appeared a fitting one for describing with some particularity

---

* *The name Concordian for a St. Paul's boy is in conformity with good usage. The pupils of St Mary's, Winchester, are known as Wintonians, from the city; those of Eton, as Etonians; of Harrow, as Harrovians; of St. Peter's, Radley, as Radleians. In the same way, instead of the rather awkward expression, a St Paul's boy, the name Concordian will be found more convenient. The boys of St Paul's School, London, are called Paulines. But this exception to the usual English custom has probably come from the fact that there are several great schools in London and from the obvious difficulty of taking a name for the scholars from so vast a city* *what sort of a school has gradually grown up; what manifold agencies and institutions have gathered about it; how they came into being, and what ends they serve.*

Almost of necessity certain persons have been spoken of freely, and the parts which they have taken in the work have been dwelt upon at some length, because the history would not otherwise be intelligible or just. It has been a pleasure to record the generous gifts St. Paul's has received in past years and to acknowledge the debt she owes to those whose talents and labors have been the chief instruments in producing the present results. How could the tributes of due appreciation be withheld when the natural opportunity for offering them was presented!

The names of all who have in any positive way aided the progress of the school would gladly have been given had the plan of the sketch permitted this.

Ab paucis disce omnes.

Concordians will not object to any of the examples which have been taken. The only regret will be that so many others who have been warm and true friends of St. Paul's in word and deed have received no special mention.

It is right to add that whatever expressions of regard and esteem for particular persons are found in the following pages appear without the knowledge or consent of those con-

cerned; no one is in any sense responsible for them but the writer; they set forth his own sentiments and feelings. But he rejoices to believe that they will be heartily and cordially approved by all who are familiar with the history of the school.

A short account has been given of the system of education pursued, the methods of training and discipline used, and the results aimed at. The religious customs are also briefly described. But it has not been intended to portray at all minutely the life and work at St. Paul's. The chief object of the sketch has been to call attention to the following facts:

After more than thirty years of slow growth and progress, St. Paul's School can show an honorable record of good work done for Church and Commonwealth. At the present moment it possesses those valuable traditions, customs, and agencies which are chief factors in the education which our age demands. The school has a fair equipment of the necessary buildings, a domain sufficiently ample for its purposes, and the beginning of an endowment. But for permanent prosperity and usefulness it needs additional buildings and appliances, and an endowment fund at least five times as large as that it has now. That St. Paul's has not been unworthy in the past of the generous benefactions and aid already received is the ground on which those who are most deeply interested in the school's welfare rest their hope that old friends and new friends will combine to make the future secure, and will gladly see that the fruits of laborious services and sacrifices, of loyal and wise devotion to the highest ends of education, of munificent gifts and foundations, shall not only be preserved, but shall be bettered and augmented for the benefit of posterity.

The writer may be permitted to claim an adequate knowledge of his subject. A residence of more than twenty-five years at St. Paul's, and an active share in the work which has been going on there, have made him very familiar with the facts and details which he records.

J. H. C.

NEW YORK CITY, *January* 14, 1891.

II.

In the year 1855 the Legislature of New Hampshire passed an act to incorporate St. Paul's School. The act was approved by the Governor on June 29th of the same year, and took effect from that date. Horatio Southgate,[*] Newton E. Marble,[†] Nathaniel B. Baker,[‡] William F. Otis,[#] Isaac F. Redfield,[‖] Matthew Harvey,[△] Jacob Carter,[◊] William E. Coale,[‡] Henry M. Parker,[‡] their associates and successors, were made a body politic and corporate by the name of St. Paul's School, and by that name it was enacted, "they may sue and be sued, prosecute and defend to final judgment and execution, and shall have and enjoy all the powers and privileges and be subject to all the liabilities incident to corporations of a similar character."

---

[*] Formerly missionary bishop in the Turkish Empire, and at the time rector of the Church of the Advent, Boston, Mass.

[†] Rector of St. Paul's Church, Concord, N. H.

[‡] Secretary of State of New Hampshire.

[#] Distinguished citizen of Boston.

[‖] Chief Justice of the Supreme Court of Vermont.

[△] Chief Justice of the Supreme Court of New Hampshire.

[◊] Prominent citizen of Concord.

[‡] Physician and devoted Churchman of Boston.

[‡] Prominent lawyer of Boston.

The trustees above named were personal friends of Dr. Shattuck, and heartily approved his plans and purposes. The act of incorporation restricts the number of trustees to eleven, and empowers them to fill any vacancies in their body. Five members present at a meeting constitute a quorum for the transaction of all business except the election or removal of the principal of the school. The principal must be elected or removed by a majority of the whole number of trustees. The corporation was permitted to acquire and hold by gift, bequest, or otherwise, real and personal estate to an amount not exceeding one hundred thousand dollars,* to erect suitable buildings, employ proper teachers and assistants, establish all necessary by-laws and regulations, and to exercise any other powers proper to carry into effect the object of its creation.

The first meeting of the corporation was held at Dr. Shattuck's residence in Concord, on the 5th and 6th days of September, 1855. All the nine grantees were present. The two vacancies in the board were filled by the election of the Right Rev. Carlton Chase, Bishop of New Hampshire, and the Hon. Samuel H. Huntington,† of Connecticut. A deed of gift from Dr. Shattuck and his wife, conveying to St. Paul's School,

---

* By an act passed by the Legislature in 1873, "St. Paul's School may acquire by gift or otherwise and may hold real or personal estate not exceeding in value five hundred thousand dollars."

† Judge Huntington was a well-known lawyer and Churchman, a prominent member of General Conventions, and an influential citizen in his State.

under certain conditions, three pieces of land situated on opposite sides of the road running from Concord to Dunbarton, containing in all about fifty-five and one third acres, together with certain buildings, was presented and accepted. The buildings consisted of a large dwelling house, a grist mill, saw mill, miller's and farmer's cottages. The conditions under which this gift was received were as follows:

1. The property is never to be mortgaged for any debt or loan, or any other purpose.

2. The members of the corporation must always be communicants of the Protestant Episcopal Church in the United States of America.

3. The religious education of the scholars must be in conformity with the doctrines, discipline, and worship of the same Church.

At this first meeting it was voted that the title of the principal of the school should be Rector. An election of a rector was also made, and Mr. Roger S. Howard, of Bangor, Maine, was chosen.

The property given to St. Paul's School at this time was intended to provide a site and temporary accommodations for the new establishment. Among the buildings was Dr. Shattuck's summer residence. The house had been originally a homely structure, known as the Brick Tavern. But it had been enlarged and transformed by many improvements, so as to become a commodious and comfortable dwelling. In this building, after certain repairs had been made and the necessary furniture supplied, St. Paul's School was to begin its life. The grist mill and saw mill would, it was hoped, produce a useful although small addition to the income, and the land would furnish garden spots and play-grounds. This first gift was only the starting point of large hopes and designs. It provided a convenient home where the enterprise could take root and under generous guardianship have prosperous growth. The founder's purpose was to give liberally during the early years of the school's existence toward its needs, and to further its expansion and improvement when the proper opportunities occurred.

The rector first chosen, Mr. Roger S. Howard, declined the offer, and at a meeting of the trustees held in Boston, January 15, 1856, the Rev. Henry A. Coit, then a missionary in Clinton County, northern New York, was elected rector. Mr. Coit accepted the office. He was married early in the spring to Miss Mary Bowman Wheeler, of Philadelphia, and arrived with his wife at Concord on the 3d of April. The school was opened at once with three pupils present.* Other boys came in, and the number of scholars soon exceeded ten. It was, of course, the day of small things, but the outlook was very encouraging. Applications were made for all available accommodations, and the boys received in the first months, as well as those for whom places were sought, belonged to families of excellent social position, and the favor and approval of these families were elements of future enlarged success.

---

* George B. Shattuck, Horatio Bigelow, and Frederick C Shattuck, of Boston.

The new rector and his wife were in hearty sympathy with the founder. The management of the school, from the day of opening, had for its inspiration the fulfilment of the noble purpose expressed in the deed of gift. "We are desirous," said Dr. Shattuck, for himself and in behalf of his wife, "of endowing a school of the highest class for boys, in which they may obtain an education which shall fit them either for college or business, including thorough intellectual training in the various branches of learning, gymnastic and manly exercises adapted to preserve health and strengthen the physical constitution, such æsthetic culture and accomplishments as shall tend to refine the manners and elevate the taste, together with careful moral and religious instruction."

It was during these first months of the school's history that the words of S. Augustine, now so familiar to all Concordians, were taken as the motto best expressing the motive and end of the work proposed to be done:

"Ea discamus in terris quorum scientia perseveret in cœlis." On a fly-leaf in the front part of the first volume of the Rural Record (a journal of weather and of the daily events in the school life, begun in 1857 and continued until 1880), the rector wrote: "'Da mihi quod jubes, Deus meus, et jube quod vis.' S. Aug. The words contain the whole system of St. Paul's." Persons familiar with the history of Dr. Shattuck's foundation will readily agree that this last quotation from S. Augustine carries in it the principle by which those chiefly concerned in building up the work were governed. They looked upon the school as work for God; they sought his favor and guidance upon all that was done and planned; without his blessing they had no hope of true success. And that deep religious spirit which marked the beginning has fixed a sort of distinct stamp upon all the after years of change and progress. Among the influences contributing to make what is called the tone or moral atmosphere of the school, the most powerful and efficacious has been the persistent recognition of the fear and love of God as the firm and lasting basis of character, as supplying the strongest motives to resist evil and do duty, and as leading on to the chief virtues and graces. This principle has pervaded the long administration of thirty-five years under one head, and, by its means, a high standard of conduct and character and a steadily good tone have been maintained.

The rector was soon joined by two assistants. One, Mr. Copeland,* of Boston, remained only a few months; the other, the Rev. Francis Chase,† a son of the bishop of the diocese, was, from 1857 until 1862, the able and faithful associate of the head master. There is a great difference between the school order of a day in June, 1856, when only a dozen boys composed the household, and the order which now regulates the day for three hundred boys. During the summer session of 1856 the rising bell was at 5 A. M.; prayers at

---

* Mr G. W. D. Copeland took holy orders a little later, but died a few years after leaving St. Paul's

† The Rev. F Chase resigned his mastership and became rector of St. Luke's, Charlestown, N. H., in 1864. After several years of successful work in Charlestown he removed to New York and took charge of the parish in Scarsdale, where he still resides.

5.45; breakfast at six. The study hours were from seven until 1.30 P. M., broken by fifteen minutes intermission at nine and a half-hour at eleven. The dinner hour was 2 P. M. The afternoon was free for recreation. Tea came at 6.30 P. M., and there was an evening study hour from eight to nine.*

The school year was at first divided very differently from the way which has been followed since 1863. The year began December 1st, and until 1860 the boys spent Christmas at the school. There was a fortnight or three weeks' recess in the spring, and the closing day fell in the latter part of October. In 1860 the opening was November 1st; a week's recess was given at Christmas, a break of two weeks was allowed in April, and the session closed at the end of August. About 1864, what was nearly the present arrangement of the year was finally settled upon. The session opened in the first part of September, and closed in the last week of June. A period of four weeks, beginning just before Christmas and extending into the third week of January, took the place of the spring recess.

The decade following the first opening was necessarily a time of germination. There were many arrangements of the details of school life which had to be tested before their value

---

* The order of the day has not varied much during the last fifteen years. Now (1891) the rising bell rings at 7.30 A. M. Breakfast is at 8; prayers, at 8.45. The morning study hours extend from 9 to 12.45, with two intermissions of five minutes each. The dinner hour is 1.30 P M. The afternoon study hours are from 4.45 P. M. to 6.40, with a break of five minutes. Tea is at 6.50 P. M., and there is an evening study hour from 7.35 to 8.45.

or suitableness could be decided. The methods which have gradually come into use are a growth from the trials and experiences of the early years. During this same period large additions were made to the accommodations and appliances by the generous provision of Dr. Shattuck, augmented by savings from the annual income. In the spring of 1858 a wing was built on the southwest side of the house, containing a school-room and dormitory, with a lavatory in the basement. The number of places for boys was thus increased to forty. During the same year a chapel was built and furnished at the entire cost of the founder.*

This chapel was small, having seats for only sixty boys and about eighty other persons, but it was a very carefully designed structure. No pains and expense were spared to make it dignified, beautiful, and adapted to its important part in the school work. More than twelve thousand dollars was laid out upon it, and although it has been much changed by enlargement the main features of the original structure still remain and witness to the devout purpose of the founder. The corner-stone of the chapel was laid on June 29, 1858. It was used for the first time for public worship on December 5th of that year. The consecration took place on the eve of St. Paul's day, January 24, 1859. Bishop Chase, of New Hampshire, and Bishop Williams, of Connecticut, were present, with several clergy from Boston and the neighboring

---

* The dimensions of St. Paul's Chapel, before its enlargement in 1868, were: Length, 48 feet; breadth, 23 feet.

towns. Bishop Williams preached the sermon. The event was significant as presaging the permanence of the school and its rapid growth.

At the opening of the session in 1859 forty-three boys were in attendance; there were no vacancies, and applications were coming in for places to be taken months and years later. It was during the first fifteen years that many of the present school customs took their rise, and most of the clubs and societies were organized. The silver medal, which is now given by the rector on the last night of the session "for distinguished excellence in the performance of school duties," was first offered in 1857 by Governor Baker, one of the trustees, to the "best boy" in conduct, and all other respects. It was conferred that year upon John Hargate,* who had entered the school in December, 1856.† The medal has been given annually, with but one omission, in 1858, since 1857. The careers of those who have received it during the third part of a century have on the whole eminently illustrated the fairness and wisdom of

---

* The Rev. John Hargate, known, loved, and respected by all boys who have been at St. Paul's School, the devoted friend of Dr. and Mrs. Coit, was born in Manchester, England. He came with his parents to the United States in 1849. He entered St. Paul's School in December, 1856. After completing the sixth form, he became a master in 1861. He was in charge of the Lower School during eight years, from 1880 to 1887. He then removed to the Upper School, of which he has been the head for the last four years

† The change of the original title of the medal, "given to the best boy in St. Paul's School," to the present more suitable designation was made about ten years later.

the awards. The medal conferred at school has been the augury of an honorable and useful life in the years that have followed.

The founder's birthday, July 23d, was observed as the school *fête* day as long as the session included July; but after 1862, when July was thrown into the summer vacation, a day in the early part of June was taken as founder's day. What is now called briefly "Anniversary" is really a celebration of Dr. Shattuck's birthday, including a commemoration of the founding of the school, at a time as near to the actual date as can be conveniently arranged.

S. Paul's day, January 25th, was also made a special holiday until 1863. In that year the winter recess was lengthened to some day between January 20th and January 25th, and it was found impossible to keep up this custom.

A gymnasium, with bowling alley, was built by the founder at the same time that the other improvements were made, in 1859, and for nineteen years it contributed largely to the physical development and to the health and pleasure of the boys. The building is yet standing, having been moved at the time the new gymnasium was built to a site near the farm stables, where it is now used for a wagon shed.*

---

* All Concordians whose dates lie between 1868 and 1888, will associate both the old and new gymnasiums with the Rev. Charles A. Morrill. The tradition of his gymnastic feats will last a long time. During his twenty years' residence at St. Paul's he was a most efficient helper

Cricket was played for the first time in June, 1857. The two elevens were composed of the boys sitting on the opposite sides of a long dining-table. Base-ball had then none of the prominence which it has now, and its popularity as a game followed long after cricket had taken root at St. Paul's. In 1859 the Olympian and Isthmian Cricket Clubs were started. The Olympians changed their name at an early date to Old Hundred. The two clubs still exist, although on a far larger scale, and with better organization than when they began. Within the last two years the whole school has been divided into three athletic clubs, called Isthmian, Delphian, and Old Hundred. Each of these clubs has three cricket elevens, two foot-ball teams, besides hockey sets and base-ball nines. The school eleven has always been made up of the best players in the entire company of boys. It has a long and honorable record of contests with some of the most prominent clubs in the United States and Canada. Cricket has been successful at St. Paul's. It has a sort of right to be considered the school game on account of its long establishment, the large expenditures which have been made for it, and its excellent history thus far. The present elevens inherit fine traditions of good playing and of courteous and manly behavior in sports, and the invaluable experience which thirty years' practice of the game on the same grounds must certainly yield.

---

in the atheletic training and sports, and was greatly liked by the boys and his associates for many excellent qualities.

The original playing field was not more than three and one half acres in extent, and is the pretty tongue of land lying between the road and pond, now about to be occupied by the new Lower School and its grounds. As the school increased in numbers and enlarged its accommodations, additions were continually made to facilities for the various games and athletic exercises. When the Upper School was built, in 1869, the level meadow lying back of it became at once a play-ground, and it has until lately been the scene of the foot-ball games, and is still in use for tennis courts. The beautiful playing fields now called the "Lower Grounds" came into possession of the school in 1866. But the land remained in a rough state for a long time. It has taken fifteen years of constant work at improvement and a large expenditure of money to transform these fields into what they are now. Among the many persons who have aided in this work, three ought rightfully to be named. Mr. James C. Knox, the Rev. James P. Conover, and Mr. Godfrey M. Brinley, all of them old boys and masters, have given ungrudgingly and unweariedly time, patience, and money to bringing the playing fields into their admirable condition. Under Mr. Knox's supervision the cricket turf was laid out and the club house built. Mr. Conover has brought the adjacent grounds into excellent shape, and Mr. Brinley has raised the necessary funds for the new tennis courts, and superintended their preparation. Many generous gifts have been made to these objects by old boys, masters, parents, and friends. The

SUBSEQUENT HISTORY. 43

school has devoted to the Lower Grounds about fourteen acres of the best land it owns, and has aided the work upon them from its resources in numerous ways. The rector has always regarded the physical training of the boys as a most important part of their education, and has contributed largely by gifts and direct personal attention to the maintenance and success of the games and athletic sports.

The position of the school favors boating, swimming, and skating. Boating at first was confined to the pond which partly encircles the grounds and to the stream which is its outlet to the Merrimac River. In 1860 a large, heavy barge, named the Ariel, was put on Long Pond, which is about one and one quarter mile distant from the school, and the sixth form were allowed to row there on summer evenings. Boys who had boats of their own were permitted to take them to Long Pond, and other boys on Wednesday and Saturday afternoons rowed there in boats which they hired on the spot. On these two pieces of water, Lake Penacook, or Long Pond, and the School Pond, the boys got considerable practice, although in a desultory way. When Harvard and Yale and other colleges began their rowing contests a great enthusiasm was aroused for boating at St. Paul's, and the excitement and interest led to the formation of the Halcyon and Shattuck Clubs. They were organized and had their first boat race in 1871. A joint club house was built at this time, and the proper equipment procured. Each club had three crews, called first, second, and third respectively, the first being composed of the oldest and most skilful rowers. Altogether between forty and fifty boys composed the crews and contestants in the various races. The training at first was done under such direction as the captains, aided by some of the masters, were able to give. Many mistakes were made, chiefly in the way of too ambitious efforts and defective preliminary exercises; but as time went on boys who had left the school, and were in Harvard and Yale crews, came back to visit their companions and taught them the methods which they had learned at Cambridge or New Haven. There was in consequence a yearly improvement in training and in style, and the school followed rapidly the various changes in rowing matters which were adopted by the colleges.

The present good state of rowing at St. Paul's is due to laborious efforts kept up for a period of nearly fifteen years. Two persons must specially be mentioned whose unwearied pains have produced lasting benefits: Mr. C. T. C. White, a scholar from 1867–'75, and afterward for two years a master, was an enthusiastic boating man during his entire residence. He rowed on the Halcyon crews, raised the money for their club house, superintended its erection, and by his energy and skill brought about many improvements. The boys are also greatly indebted to Mr. L. C. Dole, who has been their teacher in gymnastics since 1878, and has been the assiduous and successful coach of the crews for the last ten years.

Boating adds greatly to the pleasure of the boys. To many of them it has been of inestimable service in the admirable physical training it has afforded. It is expensive, but experience seems to show that it is worth its cost. Every sport which trains one to obedience, to manly endurance of restrictions, and to steady exertion; which holds up an honorable prize as an incentive to arduous effort, and at the same time teaches one to take disappointment and defeat with good temper and fairness to others, has its important place in education. Certainly boating possesses these excellent qualities, and on this account it has always been favored by the authorities of the school, while constant care has been taken to keep any hurtful customs or associations from attaching themselves to it. Silver cups and other costly prizes have been presented from time to time by old boys and friends. The Halcyons and Shattucks have never wanted warm and liberal supporters, ready to aid them in all their projects and to stimulate and strengthen the improvement of the boys in boating.

It is interesting to mark at how early a day provision began to be made for cultivating the tastes of boys in what used to be called "natural history." The arrangements and apparatus for a scientific course now existing are not the results of a late departure, but have gradually become what they are from plans and efforts carried on from the earliest years of the school to the present time. Among the many gifts of the founder at the start was a small, but choice collection of minerals and a Swiss herbarium. Mr. Chase was an excellent mineralogist and botanist, and imparted his own zeal and skill in making collections of flowers and stones to many of the boys. In 1859 an excursion was made under his direction to the silver and arsenic mine in South Dunbarton. Since then how many delightful botanical and mineralogical trips have been taken to Hooksett, Grafton, and other places! How many creditable collections of flowers, minerals, and ferns have been annually offered in contests for prizes! The boys who now attend St. Paul's are fortunate in having the skilful guidance of Mr. Edward M. Parker and Mr. George W. Lay* in their pursuits for flowers and minerals.

A prize for the best collection of native wild flowers was first given in 1866, and in 1867 another prize was offered for the best collection of minerals. Since these dates both prizes have been conferred annually, and, in addition, prizes have been given for collections of ferns and woods. Great pains are always taken to have competent judges to decide on the relative merits of the collections submitted. The prizes are handsome and valuable books presented by the rector.

The collection of minerals belonging to the school is quite large, and contains many fine specimens. Old boys have taken pleasure in sending additions to it from year to year. Bishop Chase bequeathed his own cabinet, containing a very

---

* The Rev. E. M. Parker has been a master since 1880, and the Rev. G. W. Lay since 1888.

SUBSEQUENT HISTORY. 47

good set of New Hampshire minerals. Suitable rooms and cases are needed in order to preserve and make available the mineral collection. By and by, when some generous friends shall provide a fire-proof library building, places will doubtless be supplied in it for all the various collections belonging to the school.

In 1860 a room was set apart in the Miller's House as a cabinet for physical apparatus, and a small sum was expended for a few simple instruments. Lessons in natural philosophy were given occasionally, but no systematic instruction was attempted until 1865. From that time onward physics and physical geography have been regularly taught. After 1877, when Dr. J. Milnor Coit came as a master, chemistry was added to the list of subjects in the curriculum. A little later the scientific course was laid out, and, under great disadvantages, a laboratory was started. The room set apart for this purpose had few conveniences, but the energy and skill of Dr. Milnor Coit triumphed over difficulties of all sorts. Large additions were made to the apparatus, ingenuity supplied many wants, enthusiasm and unwearied patience compelled even the dull and idle to do their best. By degrees classes were trained in physics and chemistry, not only to fulfil the college requisitions for entrance but also to acquire a solid elementary knowledge of these subjects and a genuine interest in them.

The Scientific Association was formed in 1882, with the object of stimulating and assisting the boys in such scientific studies and pursuits as are within their reach. Under the auspices of this association, lectures have been delivered on astronomy, sound, electricity, anatomy, ornithology, physical geography, and geology by eminent professors. Boys have been encouraged to prepare papers on special subjects, and, where possible, suitable experimental illustrations. Expeditions to factories and workshops have been conducted, to the great profit and pleasure of those making them. Exhibitions have been given on Thanksgiving Day, divided into botanical, physical, and chemical sections, and each year containing many interesting and instructive features. The association has also provided the school with a fine collection of birds, and, through the generosity of various members, several valuable pieces of apparatus have been presented. In 1888 the new laboratory was built, partly by gifts and partly by appropriations from the school income. The appointments of this laboratory will be sufficient for the needs of the school for many years to come. But important additions are still to be made to the apparatus, in order to enlarge the range of the teaching and to make the experimental work more complete and thorough. The course of study for the scientific side of the school needs revision, and a distinct separation should be made between the curriculum arranged for boys preparing for scientific schools and that intended for boys who drop Greek and expect to pass at once from St. Paul's into business. These and other necessary changes and improvements will be made in good time.

The Missionary Society was started by the rector on its long and useful career in 1860. It was designed to assist in the moral training of the older boys, and it has from the first been an important feature of the school life. The purpose of the society is to incite its members to charitable works, to form in them the habits of giving toward the support of missions, and of doing something for the alleviation of poverty and want. Its motto, "Non nobis, sed aliis," is a terse explanation of its objects. The society is not allowed to have more than thirty active members. These members may be any boys approved by the rector and accepted by a majority of votes at one regular meeting, and confirmed by a four-fifths vote at the next succeeding meeting. It is quite evident that a boy has to pass a rather severe test before becoming a member, so that to belong to the Missionary Society has always been a coveted honor. The president is a master named by the rector. Regular meetings are held on alternate Sunday evenings throughout the year. At these meetings there are readings and addresses about missions and other kindred objects; reports are brought in, appropriations made, and the business of the society is examined and discussed. A store has been conducted for many years by the boys under the superintendence of the Rev. Mr. Conover, who has been president since 1883. At this store most of the little things needed at school can be bought.

The articles are sold at a reasonable profit, generally at a less price than is charged at Concord stores. Sleds, skates, toboggans, balls, bats, snow-shoes, lemons, pens, and the like have formed part of the stock in trade. The profits, often amounting to several hundred dollars a year, have been paid over to the Diocesan and General Missionary Boards of the Church, or to special charities, such as the suffering caused by the great fire of Charleston, or by the Johnstown floods. Besides the store, many other means are employed in carrying out the objects of the society. Sleigh-ride parties and excursions to the Shaker settlement at Canterbury are got up under its direction. Cast-off and out-grown clothes are asked for and are sent to different parts of the country. These and other like matters require much time and care for their proper management. While the ideal of such a society, like all other ideals in this imperfect world, is only partially attained, and the fervor and enthusiasm which one would fain see enlisted in behalf of the noblest objects are only rarely found, still, the results attained by the Missionary Society are most valuable and fully justify its existence. It has taught many boys to realize that their advantages impose upon them the duty of caring for those not so highly favored as themselves. It has shown them how to act charitably if they wish to do so. It has afforded excellent training in business habits, as well as cultivated the spirit of self-denial and active exertion in behalf of the sacred cause of missions.

Horæ Scholasticæ, the well-known school paper, has been conducted by the Missionary Society since its formation. The editorial board is composed of members of the society. The money received for the Horæ goes into its treasury, and the business management is under its control. Twenty-four years is a fairly long life for a paper, and the volumes of the Horæ contain a large part of the history of the school. All the *fête* days, games, celebrations, buildings, gifts, and societies of the school are described in its pages. There are very promising buddings of poetic and romantic talent to be found in the issues of every year.* Some of the editorial articles possess considerable merits of style, and now and then gleams of genuine humor can be found. The traditions regarding the conduct of the paper are most excellent in taste and character. No article has ever appeared in the Horæ which could give pain to boy or master, nor any criticism of school affairs which had the slightest tinge of a disloyal or carping temper. In later years a great deal of information about old boys has been given—the honors won by them at college, the public events in which they have been concerned, and such facts of their personal history as might be interesting to friends and acquaintances. Their marriages are now always recorded in the Horæ, and these announcements inspire the hope that at no distant day a set of four bells will be donated to the new chapel, on condition that a peal shall always be rung at the

---

* The alumni naturally feel no little pride and pleasure in recollecting that the first piece of writing ever printed by Francis Marion Crawford, one of the most brilliant novelists of the day, is to be found in the Horæ Scholasticæ of December, 1868, entitled Carpet-Baggers, and that George Pellew, the author of In Castle and Cabin, and other works, began his literary career in the same school paper. It may be added that a poem by Owen Wister, called Brothers Again, on the reunion of North and South after the civil war (delivered before the Library Association in 1877), has been considered worthy of republication in England, by Mrs Frances Anne Leigh, in a volume entitled, Ten Years on a Georgia Plantation.

noon of the wedding day of any alumnus who may give sufficient notice of the time of his marriage.

A very valuable feature of the Horæ has been the efforts made by the different boards of editors to get contributions to the paper from as many boys as possible. Prizes are offered for the best tale or poem or account of travels. As soon as it is known that a boy has any literary talent he is sought out, and his services secured for the Horæ. Occasionally a set of editors have been able to stir up a widespread interest and to enlist a large body of contributors. The poem and oration which twice a year are delivered before the Library Association are usually published in the Horæ, and since it is an honor to a boy to be chosen either library orator or poet, this custom has an excellent effect in stimulating an ambition to do worthily.

The Horæ has always been under the general superintendence of the rector, who has given both counsel and encouragement to the young editors, and, by his special care in the early years of the paper, formed the spirit and tradition of its management. The Rev. Hall Harrison[*] for several years had

---

[*] The Rev. Hall Harrison, formerly Assistant Professor of Greek and Latin in St. James's College, Maryland, became a master of St. Paul's School in 1865. He was a brilliant and successful teacher of Greek and English. No master connected with the school has ever made a deeper impression on his scholars by his talents and personal qualities. He was greatly beloved and admired, and he exerted the most wholesome influence, both in literary matters and in the formation of character. He left the school, to the great regret of trustees, masters, and boys, in 1879, to take charge of St. John's

the supervision of the paper, and under his inspiration it had a brightness and variety which have never since been surpassed. Mr. A. M. Swift* gave also most valuable assistance after he became a master.

In fact the whole school has always taken the liveliest interest in the Horæ. The contributions of the boys have been genuinely their own, neither altered nor improved by older

---

Parish, Howard County, Maryland. He received the degree of doctor in divinity from Trinity College in 1888. He is the author of a charming biography, the Life of Bishop Kerfoot, and of other books, and is a frequent and welcome contributor to various magazines and newspapers.

* Mr. A. M. Swift, a very gifted man, was a boy at St. Paul's from the fall of 1862 to the summer of 1868. He spent three years in England under the tutorship of the Rev. Derwent Coleridge, son of the poet Coleridge, and as a member of his family. He became a master in 1874, taking as his special subjects history, elocution, and English. He was highly educated and accomplished, sang delightfully, could draw and paint well, read and spoke several modern languages, and brought to the service of the school a large variety of talents and graces. His enthusiasm for the school, admiration of the rector, generous sympathy with the boys in all their pursuits, combined with many attractive qualities, made him a most valuable master. A severe illness caused his temporary withdrawal from the school in 1880, but he resumed his duties in 1881. He was married in the winter of 1884 to Miss Prouty, of Geneva, N. Y., and obtained leave of absence for a year. He was most happy in his marriage, and his friends anticipated for him a long and useful life. He was smitten with fever while in Italy, on his wedding journey, and died in Rome. The organ in the new chapel is a memorial to Mr. Swift, and is a significant witness to the warmth of his friends' affection. Mr. Swift sang in the choir during all the years of his residence at St. Paul's. Having a rich and cultivated voice, he gave great delight by his art, and he was sincerely glad to aid in making the chapel services beautiful.

hands, although the help and sympathy of their instructors have been unfailing and most useful. It is quite evident that the Horæ fulfills many valuable ends. It assists the study of English, calls forth literary talent, and excites honorable ambition; it gives a tolerably complete record of the school history; it affords to its editors admirable training in correcting proofs and in preparing copy; and, lastly, it brings in a fair profit to the Missionary Society.

In close connection with the Missionary Society, as co-operative in work of a like character, must be mentioned the Orphans' Home, situated near the school. This charity had its origin in the pity of the rector and his wife for the children in Concord and other towns of New Hampshire whom the civil war had left fatherless, or whose parents were both dead, and for whose education and care neither public nor private benevolence had as yet made any adequate provision. In the immediate neighborhood of the school scarcely any cases of extreme poverty were to be found; but these poor neglected orphans called forth the sympathy of the boys in a special manner. The boys had the blessing of delightful homes, the love and care of parents, excellent advantages of education, numberless pleasures, and hosts of friends; but in Concord, Nashua, Manchester, the chief towns of the State where they spent nine months of the year, many orphan children were growing up in vice and want. Their fathers had died on battle-fields or in hospitals, and such friends as they could look to were themselves engaged in a tough struggle for daily bread. April 4, 1866, is the date of the opening of the Orphans' Home. A house was secured at the crossing of the Hopkinton and Long Pond roads. Here a matron and about ten children were established. The people of Concord sympathized warmly with the project and contributed liberally to its various needs; but the school became at once deeply interested. The boys gave money, clothing, books, and toys. In many cases they persuaded their parents and friends to contribute to a charity which came so close to their own hearts. The present site of the home was purchased in 1868, and on its removal to its new quarters the number of children was increased and the expenses of its maintenance were necessarily enlarged. At this time sprung up the Shaker Brotherhood,* a set of four boys who devoted themselves to collecting funds from their companions for the Orphans' Home. In soliciting gifts they made all sorts of appeals, some quaint and humorous, and others direct and sober. Strange to say, these Shakers were quite popular beggars. They collected more than one thousand dollars in four years. The number of Shakers was at first four, but was afterward increased to six. The brotherhood lasted only a few years, but in that time it did good service for the home and started an excellent tradition.

The custom of having a donation day for the home began in 1869. Committees were appointed from each form to make collections. With the money thus raised, barrels of

---

* The four boys forming the Shaker Brotherhood were Charles P. Parker, Henry C. Knox, Christopher Fallon, and Frank I. Dorr.

flour, groceries, wood, sheeting, and other necessary articles would be bought; then on the appointed day, usually the Thursday after Thanksgiving, the forms would carry up on sleds or in wagons their contributions.

Each form had an allotted hour for making its visit. At the home the boys were given refreshments, then they were conducted over the building, and were brought at last to a room where the orphans recited pieces and sang hymns for their edification. The present size of the school prevents the retention of some of these customs. The gifts of the forms are now taken to the home on donation day by committees numbering four and five, and are generally made in cash. The boys give generously, as they ought to do. A few of the alumni send every year contributions to mark their continued interest. The number of children now supported at the home is about thirty. A large brick building has lately been erected, the beginning of a series of permanent and suitable structures by which, in course of time, it is hoped to replace the old farm house and its adjuncts where the work has so long been carried on.* Until 1874 the Orphans' Home was supported chiefly by the school and was managed by the rector and his wife, aided by friends in Concord. As long as Mrs. Coit lived she guided and directed the internal manage-

---

* The Home has received several legacies from benevolent citizens of New Hampshire. The cost of erecting the new brick building, a sum exceeding $9,000, was principally defrayed from these funds. At present there is an endowment of about $11,000.

ment of the home. To her pity for the destitute children its founding was mainly due. Her sympathy and care for the work continued even when sickness and failing powers made every exertion painful. In 1874 the rector transferred the property of the home to a board of trustees named in an act of incorporation, and the institution became a diocesan one. The pastoral care of its inmates remains with the rector. Many of the supplies, ordinary repairs, the labor which must be done by men, and help in sickness, are furnished by the school. One of the masters is chaplain and treasurer of contributions for current expenses. The fact that the home has become an establishment belonging to the diocese has not diminished the interest of the boys. They recognize their obligations to contribute to the relief of poverty and misfortune, when they have the opportunity, as promptly as ever.

The Shaker Brotherhood led on to the formation of the much more important association known as St. Paul's Guild. The boys who formed the brotherhood were the first members of the guild.

In a great community of boys place may be found for very many agencies, each being used to accomplish certain specific ends, but all working harmoniously together for the edification of the whole body. School life has many sides, and the full and healthy development of a boy's character requires manifold influences to be applied. The finer and better traits of human nature do not, as a rule, burst forth spontaneously. They must be elicited by proper nurture and by presenting occasions for their exercise. The guild was primarily designed to train boys to care for one another quite independently of social position or attractive qualities. The members professed to be bound together in a sort of league to help on right and good things in the school. They were to encourage each other to the pursuit of a high standard of conduct, and they were to do everything in their power to aid their companions in their efforts to do well. For obvious reasons the success of a society formed for such objects would depend very much upon the sincerity and naturalness of its members. Boys are quick in discovering prigs, and they dislike them very much. They find out by a sort of instinct when professions are real and when they are sham. For a while the guild struggled against prejudices, arising partly from misunderstanding and partly from unwise zeal in some of the members, but by degrees the scope and intention of the society have come to be appreciated in the school, and of late years it has done excellent work in a quiet way and has had the firm support of the most influential and respected boys. Among the objects intrusted to it are the doing of kindly offices for those sick at the infirmary, the management of the Sunday library and reading room, the care of the chancel, and many other like things. In all they do they strive "to provoke one another to love and good works" and to keep up a manly, upright tone in the community. The motto of the society, τὸ καλοκἀγαθόν, is a pithy condensation of St. Paul's rule: "Whatsoever things are true, whatsoever things are honest, whatsoever things are just, whatsoever things are pure, whatsoever things are lovely, whatsoever things are of good report, think on these things . . . and these things do." A society whose ideals and aims are as high as those of the guild can not fail to be a powerful influence for good if kept under wise control.

In the first Statement of the school, issued in 1858, it was announced that a library of 350 volumes under the management of the boys themselves had been formed. The same announcement was repeated in the statements of the following five years with changes in the number of books. In 1860 there were 400 volumes, and in 1863 the number had grown to 612. The founder and the rector made many additions to the collection, and great care was taken to supply books which would be interesting and attractive and to bring within reach of the boys some of the celebrated works of literature. From the first the library was intended not only to furnish entertainment, but also to form and cultivate good taste in reading and to aid special studies and inquiries. One department which formerly belonged to the library was a collection of books for Sunday reading. This collection dates from the opening of the school, and has always had particular attention and care from the rector, and most of the books contained in it are his gift. At present there are about five hundred volumes in the Sunday library. The books are of quite varied kinds. A large number of them are stories by such writers as Miss Yonge, Mrs. Molesworth, Mr. Crake, and Mr. Church; others are biographies, records of mission work, travels, and histories. Many of the publications of the Society for Promoting Christian Knowledge are to be found on the shelves; there are besides several excellent works on Church history and on doctrinal subjects, intended for the benefit of older persons. Altogether the Sunday library serves a most useful purpose in giving access to books suitable for any day, but especially appropriate for Sunday. The annual statements after 1863 contain no further notices of the library. Owing to want of proper accommodations and systematic care the state of the library was very unsatisfactory for four or five years—from 1864 to 1870. There was, however, some progress in the way of increase, and many plans for making the collection more useful and available were discussed. At last, in 1873, a proper place was assigned for it in the new school-house. It was one of the many strokes of good fortune which have befallen St. Paul's that at this time among the masters was one with a rare knowledge and enthusiastic love of books. The Rev. Hall Harrison had the care of the library intrusted to him when it was removed to its new quarters. The occasion and opportunity were seized to organize the library in such a way as to secure the interest and pride of the school in its behalf and to make it an effective agency in the literary culture of the boys. Mr. Harrison was warmly seconded in his plans and efforts by the rector and masters. Through the generous gifts of friends the new room was furnished with suitable cases, closets and drawers, receptacles for portfolios and atlases, tables, chairs, and all the most necessary apparatus. The brown-paper covers were stripped off the books, worn-out volumes were rebound or replaced. All were numbered and labelled anew and arranged on the shelves in the sections to which their subjects belonged. Mr. Harrison imparted his own enthusiasm to the boys.

A Library Association was formed, and began its career under the happiest auspices. Any boy becomes a member of the association by payment of one dollar a year, and is entitled to take out one book at a time and to retain it for two weeks. By payment of a dollar and a half a year he may take out two books and keep them a fortnight, but only one of these books may be fiction. A fee of three, four, or five dollars a year gives the privilege of taking as many books for the space of two weeks as the number of dollars paid. A member of the association has also the use of the library as a reading room in the afternoons when it may be open for this purpose. The care and government of the library are intrusted to an executive committee. This committee consists of the librarian, who is a master, selected for this office by the rector, and who, as president of the association, has the control of its affairs; two vice-presidents, who are also masters; twelve assistant librarians, appointed by the president, generally from the three upper forms; and a number of delegates, elected by the forms above the second. The chief officers of the executive committee are the president and the first assistant librarian, who is a boy, usually belonging to the sixth form, chosen by the president on account of special fitness, and having, under the direction of the president, a general charge of the library. The committee have control of all matters connected with the care and purchase of books and periodicals; they also provide for classifying and cataloguing them. They arrange for the opening of the library, the supervision of the reading room, the registering of books lent, and replacing them in their proper places when returned. They meet on the first Saturday of each month, to hear and act upon reports and to attend to such business as may be brought before them. If success is the best proof of a wise undertaking, certainly the Library Association has justified its existence. The boys are not only interested in the library, but proud of it. They give cheerfully time and labor to carrying it on, and they have an honorable ambition to do their parts well. Some of them have proved very competent librarians, and all who belong to the executive committee get excellent training in the knowledge of books and in habits of order and precision. The Rev. Mr. Harrison was president of the association from the time of its founding until his departure in 1879. The number of books increased during that period from about one thousand to over three thousand. It is interesting to note in the Horæ of those years the constant acknowledgments of gifts of books from alumni and from boys at the school. Sums of fifty dollars, one hundred dollars, and other amounts were also given occasionally, to be expended either for books or in supplying new furniture and conveniences.

The holding of two public meetings annually began under Mr. Harrison's direction. At these meetings a report is read showing the total number of books at date, the additions by gift and purchase since the last meeting, how many books under the respective heads of fiction, history, biography, and travels have been taken out by the members of each form during the half-year, and usually offering suggestions as to the improvement of the library and keeping up interest in it. After the reading of this report literary exercises follow. Two boys, chosen by the executive committee some months before, deliver, the one a poem and the other an oration. Care is taken to select for poet and orator boys who have suitable talents. As these public meetings are held during the March and June examinations, the audience consists not only of a large part of the school, but also of trustees, visitors, and parents. The occasions call for the best efforts of the young speakers, and they spare no pains to do well. An address by the president formerly concluded the exercises; now an alumnus is invited to speak on some appropriate topic. Among the sixteen hundred alumni there are many men whose professional pursuits and experience make them competent and instructive speakers. The addresses of the alumni on these occasions have been uniformly good, and some of them have reached a high order of merit. They are always listened to by the boys and their old masters with warm interest and appreciation. The invitation to deliver such an address is really a token of regard and esteem. The cordial responses made to the invitations and the admirable addresses delivered are gratefully acknowledged as tributes of affection to their school from men whose remembrances of the days spent at St. Paul's are both kindly and lasting. The executive committee have also an annual supper in the spring. The supper is a feast of good things for mind and body. A bountiful repast is provided, and, after an hour devoted to it, toasts are proposed and responded to. The speakers, both masters and boys, are notified beforehand that they will be called upon, so that there are rarely any embarrassing breakdowns. Some of the boys rise to the occasion and speak with readiness and wit. The audience is not critical, and the evening passes away very pleasantly. The supper fulfils several valuable ends by uniting the workers for the library in agreeable association and by affording a favorable opportunity of speaking about the school and its interests.

Mr. Harrison was succeeded as president by Mr. Charles S. Knox, who has admirably discharged the duties of the office. The progress of the library under Mr. Knox's care has been most gratifying. In 1888, when the school-house was enlarged, a spacious apartment was designed and prepared for the library. The room in which it had been placed in 1878 had become too small, and the occasional use of this room for recitations, although limited as much as possible, was very objectionable. The new room will for several years to come be sufficient for the accommodation of the library. It has ample space for twelve thousand volumes. It is admirably lighted and the ventilation is excellent. As a reading room it holds twice as many boys as the former one. But pictures and curiosities and the large atlases and portfolios, which are gradually accumulating, will soon need better arrangements than can be provided now. Perhaps, when the new Lower School is finished, one of the adjacent class rooms can be spared for an addition to the library; or, better yet, perhaps before long it will come into the heart of some alumnus or other friend to build an ample fire-proof house, with rooms for all the collections belonging to the school.

Several features of the library have grown up and been greatly developed under Mr. Knox's management. The first and most important one is the reference department. This collection, now amounting to several hundred volumes, is already very valuable and useful. It contains the great English dictionaries, the principal encyclopædias (such as Appletons', Johnson's, and the Britannica), the new dictionary of English biography, excellent French, German, and Italian dictionaries, commercial and scientific dictionaries, and a quantity of hand-books and manuals on various subjects. It provides a really fine apparatus, conveniently arranged for use in all sorts of inquiries, and affording to masters and boys essential help in general literary work and also in special studies. Other improvements are placing tables in a few of the alcoves, gathering on special shelves all books relating to Shakespeare and to the particular play named as the subject of the prize in English literature for the year, and putting together by themselves such works as should be read or referred to in preparation for the English composition prize. Another addition to the usefulness of the library, now in preparation, is a complete and serviceable catalogue. The number of books at present exceeds six thousand. The annual increase, due largely to gifts and partly to purchases made from the funds provided by fees and fines, amounts to about five hundred volumes. The expenses for rebinding, subscriptions to periodicals, printing, and repairs are considerable, and use up a large part of the regular funds. The library must therefore depend for its growth and for the most important and necessary additions to it upon the continued and generous interest of the boys and alumni.

The Library Association for a while held occasional meetings for debates on selected questions. These exercises stirred up among a few boys of literary turn a desire to form a society entirely devoted to practice in essay writing, elocution, debating, and the like. In the fall of 1884 a set of six boys were permitted to organize an association for these purposes. They gave to their fraternity the name Cadmean, and it pursued a very modest career for several months; but in 1886 it was recognized as one of the regular school societies, and its value and importance have since been unquestioned. The meetings are held on alternate Friday evenings, and are devoted strictly to literary exercises. A poem, essay, miscellaneous article, and recitation are prepared for one meeting of the month. A committee appointed by the president at the beginning of each term assign their parts in these literary exercises to different members and report on the merits or defects of the various performances. A debate is also held once a month. A censor keeps the speakers from wandering from the question and brings in at the ensuing meeting a critical account of the exercise. Prizes are given for the best poem, essay, and miscellaneous article read at any of the meetings during the year. The best debater has also a prize awarded to him. Two public meetings are held in each session. At these meetings a poem, essay, and miscellaneous article are read by their respective authors and a debate follows. In June, just before the end of the term, the Cadmeans wind up the events of the year with a supper. The number of members is limited to twenty-five, taken chiefly from the three upper forms.

The Library and Scientific Associations, together with the Cadmean Society, embrace in all about one hundred boys, and offer to them considerable scope for the exercise and cultivation of special talents. They have evidently a large and important part in the education which St. Paul's gives.

There are several other clubs connected with different sports and amusements. A few years ago a chess club* had a vigorous life, held meetings, solved puzzles, and carried on tournaments. It has been revived lately with great success, and among its present members are several promising players. In past years many excellent and enthusiastic young chess players have been formed and trained by the practice which this club has afforded.

The Athletic Association gets up the sports for the field day in October, for the Easter exhibition, and for the anniversary. Its members collect the money for the prizes, settle the handicaps, arrange the events, appoint the judges, see

---

* The Morphy Chess Club was founded by the Rev. Mr. Drumm, who is himself a skillful player of the game; but it is scarcely fair to mention Mr. Drumm's name in connection with chess only. He has been a master since 1874, and is an able and successful teacher. His long and faithful services are highly appreciated at St. Paul's.

that the track is in good order, and attend to all the necessary preparations. The executive committee, composed entirely of boys, have serious duties laid upon them, and they discharge these duties very well. They are aided by several of the masters, who contribute from their own experience at school and college helpful suggestions and counsel. The athletic sports have under this management thus far been most creditable, unmarred by any bad feeling, and often distinguished by remarkable achievements.

The Racquet Court Club, as its name denotes, owns and conducts the racquet courts. Through the exertions of Mr. James P. Conover, the master who has done so much for the equipment and organization of all the athletic sports at St. Paul's, aided by an enthusiastic set of boys, the necessary funds for the racquet courts were raised in 1878. The building which was erected at that time is a wooden one, and the plans for it were furnished by an architect of Montreal who had made the designs for a similar structure in that city. The original building cost about thirty-one hundred dollars, but more than fifteen hundred dollars have since been expended in improvements and in the addition of the squash-ball courts. The inadequate dressing room and the poor bathing facilities are great defects. The heating arrangements are also bad, and on cold days neither the galleries nor dressing room can be kept sufficiently warm.

But, notwithstanding the rudeness of its furniture, the lack of conveniences, and other drawbacks, the racquet court is a very flourishing institution. In the winter it supplies its fifty members with vigorous exercise in a delightful pastime, and a goodly number of fine players have acquired in it their knowledge and skill. To become a member of the racquet court an initiation fee of ten dollars is paid; there is an annual tax besides of one dollar. The squash-ball courts, four in number, are intended to give training for the racquet courts. Any boy by the payment of twenty-five cents a year acquires the right of using them. Two tournaments are held during the session, one near Christmas and the other at Easter. The names of the senior and junior championships in these contests are inscribed on tablets placed in the hall of the racquet court. It is to be hoped that a brick building with four courts, with suitable dressing rooms and bathing conveniences, will eventually replace the rough but serviceable racquet courts which have been the scene of so much healthful pleasure and exercise in the twelve years of their existence. The need of a larger, better built and furnished structure is yearly becoming more pressing. A half-dozen fives' courts could be arranged for at the same time without great additional cost.

In those dreary seasons of the year when but little pleasant outdoor exercise is possible, racquet and fives' courts, having accommodations enabling seventy or eighty boys to play in the course of an afternoon, would be of the greatest service to health and happiness. Whenever an alumnus who has the means and inclination wishes to confer some great and permanent benefit on the school he can realize his purpose by building and equipping new racquet and fives' courts.

Mention should also be made of the Mechanical Club, which, although only three years old, has already supplied an important means for the cultivation of certain special talents of boys. It was started by Mr. A. H. Campbell, the present curator, who, being himself an accomplished and experienced mechanical engineer, has devoted time and skill liberally to the organization and direction of the club. The rector provided funds for building a workshop, and the boys and their friends gave the money for the necessary tools and machines. Altogether eleven hundred dollars have been expended on the equipment. An experienced mechanic teaches the boys how to use the tools and other appliances, and superintends their work. Thus far the management of the shop has not been formally undertaken by the school, but the need has arisen of more systematic control, in order to prevent boys undertaking constructions beyond their skill, and to secure adequate training in the elementary parts of mechanical work. Only boys with decided tastes and aptitudes for using tools and machines have as yet been allowed to belong to the club. But so good a beginning has been made that the day is not far distant when all who take a scientific or commercial course will have lessons and practice in the workshop as part of their training. Whether mechanical teaching will by and by be furnished to any large portion of the school will depend partly on the possibility of having sufficient time for it along with the studies which a boy is obliged to take up, and partly on a master being opportunely found able to organize and direct it to the real profit of the pupils. Of course,

SUBSEQUENT HISTORY.

whenever the day for such extended arrangements comes, a large outlay will be required in order to supply the class rooms and apparatus for this kind of teaching.

In the enumeration of the various societies and clubs which have sprung up at St. Paul's, and which supply so many influences in training and forming the character of the boys, one remains still to be described—one which has connected with it a host of pleasant memories, and which has long been the pride and delight of the school. The choir can not with strict propriety be called a society, yet its members are bound together more closely, and certainly more harmoniously, than those of most clubs. For twenty-two years the instruction and training in vocal music have been given by one person. In 1868, while the enlargement of the old chapel was in progress, the Sunday services were held in a room in the second story of the building now called "Number Three." There the present choir master and organist began his long and valuable services to the school. A cabinet organ was his first instrument, and a company of ten boys composed the choir. But Mr. James C. Knox had even then, although a very young man, a rare enthusiasm for music, natural and kindly tact as a teacher, and refined taste. He spared no efforts to perfect himself as a musician, and he expended almost unlimited patience and time in training the choir. He imparted a portion of his own ambition and zeal to his pupils and colaborers. The boys cheerfully gave both study and play hours to practising, although no release from the regular school work was ever gained thereby. The custom, now so valued and so edifying, of singing on Sunday morning, just before the beginning of the communion office, an anthem which has been carefully prepared, and which is the composition of some well-known author, began in a modest way in the homely room used as a temporary chapel in 1868. Since then great improvements have taken place in style and method, and good material is far more abundant. But the influences which have made the choir so uniformly good have been throughout the devotion and skill of its master, upheld by the unfailing sympathy of the rector. When it is remembered that every year witnesses many changes in the *personnel* of the choir, due partly to boys leaving the school and partly to the physical alterations in the quality of young voices, it can be understood what incessant labor and care are required to keep up a sufficiently large and capable body of singers. The work of training and drilling in the rudiments of the vocal art never ceases. At the beginning of each school year, and from time to time during the term, new members come into the choir, most of whom must be taught the a, b, c of vocalization. The long winter and summer vacations make no little havoc with results which have cost a great amount of labor and patience to obtain, and much of the drill in the fall has to be repeated after the Christmas recess. The work done by masters and boys who are members of the choir is entirely voluntary, given often from a natural delight in singing, given sometimes from a generous sentiment and the willingness to contribute to the pleasure and benefit of others, and now and then given from a high sense of duty, combined with regard for the choir master and sympathetic interest in his task. There never have been any special favors or privileges granted to the choir. The boys belonging to it have always been expected to do their regular duties without exception, and, as an actual fact, many of them are most industrious and successful scholars. A holiday in the summer term, and one or two moderate festivities during the fall and winter, have been the only special gratifications allowed. The result of this treatment has been the formation of a fine *esprit*. The boys are glad to belong to the choir. They take pleasure in learning difficult anthems, chants, and hymn tunes for the chapel services. They prepare for their musical contests, anniversary and last-night concerts with genuine zest and enthusiasm. They are thoroughly pleased, and feel themselves rewarded when they know that they have done their tasks well; when the musical parts of divine service have been rendered so as to edify and delight; when the concerts have gone off successfully, and their parents and friends, who are frequently critical judges, express satisfaction and approval. Injudicious praise will often seriously injure the character of a boy who has a charming voice. But the spirit of the choir management at St. Paul's has, on the whole, successfully checked this evil. Rarely does one notice in a boy who has a specially fine voice any conscious attempt to display it, or any obtrusive conceit on account of his gift. It is quite evident that the choir training confers great benefits on all whom it reaches. Nowadays there are the vocal-music classes, for which, at last, a proper room and regular hours are provided. These classes contain between thirty and forty of the boys in the first and second forms. There are besides several practisings each week of the basses, tenors, and altos, and two full rehearsals. Altogether, from fifty to sixty boys receive instruction in vocal music during the year. They are taught to produce their voices properly, and in most cases to read music correctly. But the greatest advantages come to them from the lovely influence of music itself, the habits of attention and unselfishness which are cultivated, and the refined taste which is formed by the pieces which they learn to sing, and the association of older and younger in a common work, where there is no place for petty rivalries and jealousies.

More than three hundred boys have belonged to the choir in the last twenty years, and, without exception, the old members testify in numberless ways to the regard in which they hold it and the pleasant recollections of it which they have.

Among the many endowed with delightful voices who in years gone by have been ornaments of the choir and by their love of music, loyal devotion to the school, and cordial co-operation were invaluable helpers of Mr. Knox in his various efforts and plans, one recalls with pleasure—

> FRANK H. POTTER, 1867–'71.
> GEORGE R. SHELDON, 1868–'75.
> AUGUSTUS M. SWIFT, 1862–'68.

WILLIAM F. JENNISON, 1877-'82.
HOFFMAN MILLER, 1871-'76.
GEORGE S. HODGES, 1881-'86.

If, however, a complete list was given of all the boys whose vocal gifts and generous tempers during the existence of the choir have been its life and strength, several pages would be required. One can not but wish that a much larger number of boys could have training in vocal music than now receive it. Such training has so refining an influence and forms such valuable habits of attention, elocution, and intelligent expression that if it could be made a regular subject of the curriculum, embracing as many boys as possible, the school would reap great advantages.

Before leaving the topic of music it should be added that instruction in instrumental music is perhaps at this time more carefully arranged for than ever before. There has always been a great deficiency of rooms and instruments for practice, and a further difficulty in getting first-rate teachers at a reasonable cost. Violin and piano playing are taught now by masters coming from Boston and other cities and spending a day at the school giving lessons. Several successful bands have been formed at different times. The last one, containing wind and string instruments, made excellent progress under the guidance of Mr. Lay, and its suspension has been much regretted. It is to be wished that a band could become a permanent feature. It gives amusement and occupation to to its members and scope to special tastes. The masters who devote time to this and other like things serve the school most effectively.

From the mention of violins and pianos there is a natural passage to the organ, the noblest of all musical instruments. Four organs have been in use in the school chapels at different periods. The first, which stood in the old chapel until the time of its enlargement, was quite a small one, and is now in St. John's Church, Dunbarton. The second organ, costing about eight hundred dollars, was in use from 1868 to 1876. It is now set up in the church at Ashland, New Hampshire. Both of these organs were the gift of the founder. As the choir grew and improved, keeping pace with the enlargement of the school, the need of a much better organ became pressing. In 1878 Mr. Knox took up the matter, and through his efforts a fine new organ was procured costing eighteen hundred and fifty dollars. This instrument still occupies its original position in the old chapel. Finally, when the new chapel was built, it seemed necessary to put in an organ in keeping with the large and beautiful building and having all recent improvements of positive value. The lamented death of Mr. Swift occurring near this date, it was resolved to make the new organ a memorial to him. The choir master devoted himself to the work, and the necessary sum was raised within two years. Mr. Charles P. Gardiner, of Boston, one of the trustees, superintended the construction of the instrument and watched over every detail. His thorough knowledge, combined with excellent taste and judgment, secured an admirable result. The school has in the new chapel a noble

SUBSEQUENT HISTORY.

instrument (some good judges have pronounced it as fine as any in New England) sufficiently powerful and almost perfectly adapted to its service.

But it is time to turn back to note the expansion and growth of the school in buildings, land, and numbers since 1860.

The successive enlargements were due to the pressing applications for places, which far exceeded the accommodations. In 1863 extensive additions and alterations were made after plans furnished by Mr. Upjohn, the celebrated architect, and under his superintendence a large school room with class rooms attached was erected, a Mansard roof supplying an additional story was put on the old building, the back wing was greatly extended so as to give a new dining room, kitchens, and other conveniences, a system of drains was constructed, and many other improvements made. The number of places provided by these changes was about seventy. By putting groups of boys in the miller's and farmer's cottages and in the Shute Cottage* additional accommodations were secured, so that as many as eighty boys were received in the fall

---

* The Shute Cottage was a plain one-story farmer's house about two hundred yards northeast of the main school building. It had a number of sheds attached to it and a small triangular-shaped piece of ground. After the first opening of the school, Dr. Shattuck for two or three years spent a few weeks of the summer in this cottage, then, seeing that the addition of this property would give to the school much needed rooms, he bought and presented it to the corporation. In 1869 the sheds and barns were torn down, the cottage was raised, and a story put under it; wings were attached, and the homely, rambling structure which for twenty years has

of 1867. In that year also the house known as Number Three was built as an addition to the old gymnasium. The lower story was furnished with bowling alleys and the upper was divided into two large rooms. One of these rooms had cupboards for the apparatus and collections of the school; the other was a play room. The total expense of these various improvements, amounting to nearly ten thousand dollars, was paid in greater part by the founder. It seems proper to record that on Sunday, August 26, 1860, the founder deposited in the offertory his note for five thousand dollars, signifying that the sum was given for a new building. Two years from this date he presented to the trustees stocks and other securities to the value of $20,425, and explained in the following letter his purpose:

---

been the "Lower School" and has each year supplied places for thirty boys came into being. Eight years later a small but commodious house was added on the south side. But the days of the present "Lower School" are numbered. A large and ample building is now erecting to replace it. The designs for the new Lower School have been drawn by Mr. Henry Vaughan, and its estimated cost is about one hundred thousand dollars. More than one half of this amount has already been given by generous friends of St. Paul's. The greater part of the old Lower School will probably be removed after the new building is occupied.

It is only just to add that the erection of the new Lower School is largely due to the efforts and zeal of Dr. J. Milnor Coit. A munificent subscription of ten thousand dollars was received from Mr. Cornelius Vanderbilt, of New York, at the outset, and many gifts of one thousand dollars and of smaller sums have also been made to this object. If St. Paul's has had many needs, it has also had many large-hearted and cordial helpers.

St. Paul's School, *August* 26, 1862.

Gentlemen of the Corporation: I herewith offer you certificates of six shares in the Amoskeag Company, of six shares in the Nashua Manufacturing Company, and of one share in the Cocheco Company, which I request you to accept as a fund for two scholarships, to comply with one of the objects set forth in the deed of donation. At St. Mary's, Winchester, seventy scholarships were furnished by the founder, and perhaps the members of this corporation can do something toward supplying a want of St. Paul's School, in calling the attention of the faithful to the great importance of further provision for the gratuitous education of deserving boys whose parents are not able to maintain them at school and college. I have already given to the corporation the sum of five thousand dollars, and I propose now to convey four shares in the Cocheco Manufacturing Company and six shares in the Nashua Manufacturing Company, which I ask the acceptance of in discharge of the obligations assumed by me in the aforesaid deed of donation. I wish to modify the conditions set forth in that deed so as to allow a sum of five thousand dollars to be appropriated toward a new building, to be used for school rooms, recitation rooms, and dormitories, and a further sum of two thousand dollars, to be spent in enlarging the chapel or in otherwise providing for the spiritual wants of the school and the neighborhood. I am not satisfied with the present provision, but I leave to the corporation the responsibility of deciding at what period such work shall be commenced. I can not refrain at this time from congratulating the corporation on the success which has been vouchsafed in carrying on the work intrusted to them. A great deal has been accomplished in six years and a half, and with small and inadequate means. That those in charge of the school may be blessed and prospered in their earnest and self-denying labors for Christ and his Church, is the wish and prayer of

Your obedient servant,

GEORGE C. SHATTUCK.

The increase of the school made an enlargement of the chapel erected in 1858 necessary. Mr. William Ware, now Professor of Architecture in Columbia College, prepared the plans for the proposed changes. The rector went abroad in June, 1868, and was absent eight months. During that period the chapel was cut in two at the juncture of choir and nave; the latter part was moved to a new foundation, and a cross piece was inserted. The interior was greatly improved by these alterations, and the number of seats was more than doubled. Three hundred and thirty persons could, by crowding, be provided with places. The old chapel is to-day in nearly every respect the same as it was in 1869, when the enlargement was completed. The founder paid the entire cost of its alteration, expending about eight thousand dollars. It is his gift, and bears witness to his benevolent heart, and to the noble purposes which he wished to carry out at St. Paul's. The bell on the old chapel and the one on the school-house were both given by the founder, and have been in constant use since 1859. On the school-house bell is this inscription:

Tempus Fugit;
Ars Cogit;
Dulce Ludendum;
Bonum Studendum;
Vita Decrescit;
Futura Instat.

The enlargement of the chapel was scarcely finished before plans were on foot for a new building, with rooms for boys in the fifth and sixth forms. Mr. Ware, who had so skilfully designed the changes in the chapel, furnished the drawings, and in the fall of 1869, the erecting of the Upper School was begun. At the same time, out of the farmer's cottage and an old chair factory close adjoining, together with other rambling sheds, was constructed the main part of that queer group of buildings which still contains the dining room, kitchens, pantries, and other offices of the Upper School.* The present Lower School, with the exception of

---

* The "Upper School" is an unfinished building. It was erected shortly after the close of the civil war, when prices were very high, and its cost was heavy. To complete the Upper School properly two wings should be built; one containing additional rooms for older boys, a common room, two or three suites for masters, bath rooms, and sundry other conveniences; the other, having dining hall, kitchens, pantries, and accompanying offices, together with a matron's apartment. The interior of the present building should be entirely rearranged, and the pile of wooden structures, now used for dining room and kitchens, ought to be removed as early as possible. The existing arrangements are expensive, inconvenient, and unsuitable.

the house on the southwest side, which was built four years later, was compiled (if so odd but appropriate use of this last word may be allowed) at this time from the Shute Cottage and its various appendages.*

Here for a while twenty-four boys not only had their residence, but did their school work also. A master and his family had their home in the same house. The entire expense of these various buildings was about thirty-five thousand dollars. Toward this amount Dr. Shattuck, with his accustomed liberality, contributed six thousand dollars. Mr. John H. Swift, a trustee, and a warm friend of St. Paul's, gave also six thousand dollars. This last amount, although

---

* The Rev. Mr. Benton, an accomplished and valued master, from 1860 to 1884, now rector of St. John's Church, Sewickly, Pa., was the first head of the Lower School. He moved from it to take charge of the School in 1872, after the rectory was finished. The Rev. Hall Harrison succeeded him at the Lower School, and remained in charge until 1878. The Rev. John Hargate was head after Mr. Harrison's leaving until 1886, when Mr. J. H. Coit became his successor.

Dr. Shattuck's country-house which, with many additions, was the principal residence of the boys for twenty-two years, was called "The School." After its burning, in 1878, the large building erected to take its place, about one hundred and fifty yards due east from it, received and still bears the same name, The School. The two other main residences of the boys have been called "Lower School" and "Upper School." The building in which lessons are prepared and recited is known as "The School-House"; the boys themselves often call it "the Study." "Number Three," "Miller's," "Farm," "Hillside," are the current designations of outlying cottages occupied by groups of boys of varying numbers, the largest group reaching thirty-six, and the smallest five.

for a while diverted toward paying for these buildings in accordance with the donor's express wish, has since been given back by the school from its income and forms part of a special permanent fund known as the Swift endowment. The remaining debt of twenty-three thousand dollars was discharged in the course of three or four years by savings from the annual revenues.

One great advantage accruing from increased accommodations and a larger number of boys has been a surplus of receipts over expenses, with rare exceptions, at the close of each financial year. By careful economy and good management this result has been almost invariably secured. With this surplus many of the additions to the school property in land and buildings have been paid for entirely, and others, toward which contributions have been made, have had a part of their cost defrayed.

In 1872 the still increasing number of boys and the lack of proper class rooms and of a sufficiently large study room compelled the trustees to venture on the erection of a school-house. About the same date, Dr. Samuel Eliot, a trustee, the well-known man of letters and the widely esteemed patron of many good works, raised by his own efforts the money for building a rectory. In response to a statement sent out by him he received from parents and old boys a sum exceeding sixteen thousand dollars. Dr. Eliot secured in this way a signal benefit for the school. He had the satisfaction of seeing, within eighteen months after he began his task, a fine house built and the rector and his family established in a comfortable and suitable home.*

The new school-house reached completion almost at the same time as the rectory. The capacious study room, with ample space for two hundred boys, the six large class rooms in the upper story, and the three in the basement, the rector's office, the three suites for masters, the play room, were all absolutely needed for the work of the school. The cost of the building, including the furniture, was over forty-six thousand dollars. Again the large-hearted founder aided the school by the gift of six thousand dollars, coupling with it only the condition that two nephews, specified by name, were to receive their education at St. Paul's in discharge of the obligation. Mr. William C. Sheldon, a trustee whose interest in the school and generous aid in all its projects and needs have been unfailing, with the co-operation of a few other gentlemen, contributed five thousand dollars towards the same object. In 1888 an extension of the school-house was made, planned and directed by Mr. Campbell, the curator, giving three additional class rooms, a large and fine room for the library, and greatly improving the look of the building. The cost of this addition, amounting to ten thousand dollars, and the thirty-five thousand dollars due on the

---

* The rectory has been enlarged by an addition made to it in 1890 after plans by Mr. Vaughan. A suitable stable was built in 1886. These improvements, costing nearly nine thousand dollars were paid for from the school income.

original school-house and not discharged by gifts, were both paid out of the annual income. It was six anxious years before the larger of these two debts was entirely wiped out. The number of boys received during the session of 1871-'72 was one hundred and fifty-eight. Between 1870 and 1885 there was a steady increase, limited only by the possibility of providing accommodations. In 1874-'75 the school list contained one hundred and seventy-eight names, and in the following year one hundred and ninety-six.

In all the years down to 1876 the various ailments of the boys had been attended to under Mrs. Coit's kindly and watchful direction; but the burden grew too great along with the other cares. In 1875 a number of friends of the school contributed five thousand dollars toward an infirmary. The building was erected after plans by Messrs. Ware and Van Brunt at a cost of seven thousand dollars. It was first occupied in 1876, and Dr. Milnor Coit and his wife had their home in it for nine years, watching with self-forgetful and unwearied care over every sick boy who came there for attention. In 1888 an addition was built to the infirmary after designs by Mr. Vaughan (architect of the new chapel), which has more than doubled its capacity. This new part has been specially constructed for the complete isolation of any boys attacked by contagious diseases. It is hoped that such occasions will be few and far between.* The addition has thus

---

* There have been four outbreaks of scarlet fever at St. Paul's during thirty-five years. The same number of visitations of measles have also oc-

far been partly occupied by older boys, and is constantly used for the entertainment of alumni and other visitors. The infirmary has since 1885 been under the charge of matrons who have been competent trained nurses, and who, uniting skill with kindness, have made the sick boy's lot as comfortable and safe as possible.

Besides these principal buildings several smaller ones have been erected; old cottages have been repaired and converted to the uses of the school. The Belknap property, containing a house, large barn and sheds, with eighty-six acres of land, was bought in 1866 for six thousand dollars. The house was much enlarged in 1887, and is now known as the Farm Building, and has rooms for two masters and twenty boys besides the office of the curator. The barn was a large unsightly object situated on the brow of the hill, at the base of which stand the school-house, the two chapels, and the rectory. It was a blot on a very pretty view, and there was great satisfaction when it was removed to the spot it now occupies. It was at the same time reconstructed and has lost all traces of its former appearance. These various improvements on the Belknap property cost over ten thousand dollars. The Hillside Cottage was bought in 1874 for about three thousand

---

curred. With but one exception the diseases were brought by boys from their homes. In one instance, scarlet fever was introduced through the family of a new employé, coming from Boston during the fall session. There seem to be no precautions which can absolutely prevent the occasional appearance of such diseases in communities like St Paul's. The school must depend on the watchfulness and care of parents for its chief protection.

dollars. It has been the home in succession of three married masters, and until 1889 has also afforded rooms for a small set of boys. In 1875 two small properties, known respectively as the Howe and Rose cottages, were purchased for thirty-eight hundred dollars. Some scattered pieces of land, amounting in all to twenty-seven acres, were also bought in order to bring the estate into good shape.

The domain of the school in 1876 had by different purchases been raised from its original extent, fifty-five acres, to one hundred and eighty-five acres. The land is not very productive, but there are several good pasture tracts, and constant enriching of parts of it, together with drainage, has made the annual crops bring in a profit. However, the purpose in view in additions to the landed property has not been to increase the income or even to support the fifty or sixty cows which give the liberal quantity of milk now daily used. As soon as it was evident that a large boarding school was growing up it became necessary to surround the central location by grounds in which the boys could circulate without chance of collision with neighbors or strangers. It is a remarkable fact that during the thirty-five years of the school's history scarcely any complaints of damage or rude conduct have been brought against the boys by the farmers who live adjoining. Friendly relations have always existed between St. Paul's and its neighbors.

The care of a farm of two hundred acres requires the services of several men, and one object effected by the purchase of cottages was providing homes for the employés.

The expense of all these later additions, amounting to twenty-five thousand dollars, was defrayed chiefly from the annual income. No better proof of a wise financial management could be adduced than the sums devoted almost every year to school extension from the income and the fact that the actual cost of carrying on and keeping up the establishment has never exceeded the receipts. Whatever debts have been incurred were caused by new buildings, purchases of property, or large improvements.

In 1878 a great calamity befell St. Paul's. The old house given by Dr. Shattuck, which by many changes and additions had become a large establishment, supplying accommodations for eighty boys, was struck by lightning and burned to the ground. It had just undergone extensive repairs under the advice of the celebrated sanitary expert, Colonel George E. Waring. Very few of the buildings had up to this time been provided with lightning rods. The many tall trees in the grounds and the woods on all sides had been thought to afford ample protection. On Sunday, the 21st of July, just before morning service, there was a slight shower, at first scarcely exciting attention, and promising to last only a short time. Then came a vivid flash of lightning, accompanied by a peal of thunder, and immediately after it was discovered that the School was on fire. The flames seemed to issue from the lower edges of the roof and to follow their lines with great rapidity. As soon as the alarm was given efforts were made at once to save the property. Fire engines were sent for; furniture of every sort was removed when possible. It was soon seen that little could be done to check the progress of the fire with the means and force on hand, and nearly three quarters of an hour elapsed before help came from Concord. The flames gained headway every moment, and when at last the engines poured in their streams of water it was too late. In a little more than an hour from the first discovery of the danger the entire building was at the mercy of the flames, and only a very small part serving as a laundry was finally saved. It was the middle of vacation. Dr. Coit and his family were in New Brunswick. It can easily be imagined with what a shock the following telegrams were read by him on the next day in St. John:

"CONCORD, N. H., *July 21, 1878.*

"1. School struck by lightning this morning; now burning; engines here."

Two other telegrams of the same date were as follows:

"2. Fire out; school burned to the ground; a great deal of the furniture saved; no one hurt."

"3. School destroyed; part of contents saved; chapel and No. 3 safe; no one injured."

The first two of these telegrams were signed by the then curator, Mr. William H. Bates.* The last was sent by Dr.

---

* Mr. Bates, now a clergyman in Florida, was curator from 1874 to 1886. He was a faithful and conscientious business manager and a careful guardian of the school's property.

A. H. Crosby, for many years the able physician and devoted friend of the school.

The true test of a man, it is said, is adversity. The best traits and powers are not ordinarily brought out to their full display except under the pressure of misfortune. Certainly Dr. Coit in this trying emergency showed new capacities and force, together with a quickening of all the remarkable qualities which had distinguished his work hitherto. He returned at the earliest moment to Concord and at once set to work to prevent harm and extract good from what had happened. There were six weeks remaining of the summer vacation. After hurried consultations with builders and business men he concluded that it would be possible, even in the short time left before the fall opening, to arrange for the reception of every boy on the list. This meant, of course, the provision of quarters for the eighty boys whose places were to have been in the building which had been destroyed. Immediately a large force of mechanics was set to work erecting a new cottage, putting another story on the miller's house, turning the whole ground floor of Number Three into a dining room and the upper rooms into a dormitory; filling one class room in the school-house with alcoves, and making ready another for a master's occupancy; converting every available chamber into a sleeping room for boys, and carrying on many other necessary pieces of work. Not a few persons thought that Dr. Coit was attempting the impossible, and there were some advisers who recommended a postponement of the day of opening for two or three months. Others were quite despondent as to the future of St. Paul's, while some again were oversanguine as to the help and sympathy which the disaster would elicit. There were enthusiastic friends who expected that a simple statement of the situation would call forth funds more than sufficient to replace what had been destroyed; but the rector's clear foresight and resolute energy met the difficulties in the right way. The essential thing was to have no break in the school's progress and to show to its friends that it had the principle of life in itself and could survive a disaster, such as had befallen it, with unimpaired power for doing its work. The trustees resolved to raise money toward replacing the old by a far larger, and more perfect building. In the mean while the preparations for the fall term went on with surprising speed. When the regular day for opening arrived, the wreck and rubbish of the fire had been cleared away, the various temporary arrangements had been completed, and the school began the term of 1878-'79 with undiminished numbers and with fairly satisfactory accommodations for every pupil. Of course there were many inconveniences, and the masters cheerfully bore their share of the burden. Some gave up rooms; one offered the house which he had occupied with his family; others went into such quarters as could be found in the neighborhood. The rector had hearty support from the whole body of his co-workers, and they joined, as far as in them lay, in his determination to see that the school rose out of its trouble with every good feature and influence unharmed.

The two years that followed, while the new school was building, were very hard and trying ones. It required incessant work and care to keep up the tone and discipline to the old standards under the many disadvantages which existed. The situation was relieved in some measure by the erection of the new gymnasium, and the rising walls of a capacious and admirably planned building gave promise that this trying period would at no distant day come to an end.

The project of a new gymnasium had been started by a company of masters and boys about a year before the fire. The need of such a building for athletic training and exercises had become very great. The school had outgrown the gymnasium built twenty years before by Dr. Shattuck. Moreover that structure had but little of the apparatus and arrangements now found everywhere in such establishments. There was no way of heating it in cold weather, or of lighting it at night. The new gymnasium was therefore a most popular enterprise with the boys and their friends. An enthusiastic committee soon collected about twelve thousand dollars for this purpose. The rector appropriated four thousand dollars toward the same object. In the summer of 1878, the building was begun, and by January of the next year it was finished and ready for use. The great chamber under the roof, designed for an auditorium, was left to be completed at a future date, owing to lack of funds. It was at once made into a dormitory and served this purpose very well for two years. Since 1880, it has been devoted to its appropriate uses, and has been the scene of anniversary concerts, military drills, dances, club exercises, the Easter balls, and of many lectures and entertainments. Three thousand dollars will be needed to finish the auditorium. The walls should be plastered and painted; the roof is still to be ceiled and given suitable form; and many other things remain to be done. The gymnasium is fast becoming too small for the great company of boys who throng it during the winter months. The walking track is inconvenient; there is no room which can be set apart for practice with the rowing weights, and there is no swimming bath. Two plans for meeting these difficulties have been talked of. One is to build an addition on the northeast end, large enough to contain entrance hall and staircase, and to throw into the gymnasium room and auditorium the space occupied by the present staircase and passages. This plan would effect a great improvement, but would not increase the size sufficiently if the number of boys should reach three hundred and fifty. A second is to convert the gymnasium into a library building, and erect a new one better adapted to the present needs. But the carrying out of either plan must wait until the necessary funds are supplied by gifts.

While the new gymnasium was in progress efforts were making to get the money for a building to replace the burned one, planned and constructed with reference to its uses, embodying the experience of past years, and large enough to be the residence of one hundred and twenty-five boys. The insurance due on account of the fire, amounting according to the policies to thirty thousand dollars, was paid only after serious reductions. The sum received was sixteen thousand dollars. The insurance companies took what many thought to be an unfair advantage. On the ground that the property was not worth the amount insured, they proposed either to rebuild the house which had been destroyed, or to submit the settlement to arbitrators. Colonel John H. George, an able lawyer of Concord, well versed in such matters, was of opinion that the school should have accepted the first proposal at once. The settlement in that case would have been for the full amount of insurance, or for a sum not very much less. But the dispute was referred to arbitrators and the result was a serious loss. In addition to the insurance money, a sum of seventeen thousand dollars was received from several warm friends. But the new building together with its furniture and the grading and laying out of the grounds cost eighty-six thousand dollars. The school paid in the course of six years out of its savings forty-eight thousand dollars of this amount. The remaining five thousand dollars were provided through the efforts and liberal aid of Mr. William C. Sheldon.

It must never be forgotten that throughout the history of St. Paul's the founder has been its active and generous friend. Besides the munificent gifts already mentioned, he has contributed to many other objects. Toward the house built in 1875 for the head of the Lower School he gave three thousand dollars. There have been several other gifts from him in aid of various improvements, the total value of which makes a large sum. In all, the founder has devoted to the endowment and equipment of St. Paul's School at least one hundred thousand dollars. He has given not only properties and large sums of money, but also constant sympathy and cordial co-operation. He has been the warm personal friend of the rector from first to last, and in the long period of thirty-five years unbroken esteem and attachment have existed on both sides. It would be difficult to enumerate the countless services of good-will and kindness done by Dr. Shattuck to St. Paul's. In cases of severe sickness, he has been wont to come and give freely the benefit of his large experience and medical skill. In all emergencies he has been prompt to do everything in his power. The library has received a large number of books from him. The various collections are indebted to him for valuable contributions. He has been a frequent visitor at examinations, going with kindly interest from class room to class room, making the acquaintance of masters, and paying careful attention to the recitations. He has brought many persons to visit St. Paul's, and has sought to enlist their interest and favor in its behalf. For years he was in the habit of delivering most useful addresses to the boys on the care of their bodily health. No detail of the life and work has ever been overlooked by him. And in all these years and through all this varied intercourse his *rôle* has been that of the true and gentle friend. He has never interfered in any way with the government of the school or obtruded his preferences and wishes. He has kept himself in the background, and the purity and unselfishness of his motives have been manifest to all men. A founder so guileless, so devout and sincere, so large-minded and so unchanging in interest and regard, necessarily has had a marked influence on the history of the school. In union with himself and the rector the trustees have acted in constant harmony and with no serious differences of opinion in regard to financial matters or the general management. Men who give to schools and other institutions of learning usually do so in the form of bequests taking effect after their deaths. Few are willing to make the necessary sacrifices for such large and generous benefactions as those of Dr. Shattuck in their life-time. The account which he has given of the motives and influences which led him to found St. Paul's School shows very strikingly the high yet practical ideal of education which he had in view. Blessed is the man who sees fruit growing on the tree which has sprung from a seed that he himself planted. Dr. Shattuck has the happiness of already witnessing large results from his munificent gifts. He has every reason to hope that in the future his foundation will continue to fulfil his purpose and still more entirely than now contribute to the glory of God and the good estate of men. May his beautiful example inspire others to go and do likewise.

The New School, as it was called, was the first thoroughly adapted and furnished house erected for St. Paul's; and though the experience of ten years' use of it has shown that several features could be altered with great advantage, still

SUBSEQUENT HISTORY.

it has stood the test of trial well, and its defects are small in comparison with its merits. Its completion marked a new and firm step forward. Not only could a larger number of boys now be received than before, but the provisions for their comfort and health were more ample and satisfactory. When the Lower School, now erecting, is finished, the time will have arrived for remodelling and completing the house for the upper forms. After that is done, St. Paul's will have an adequate equipment, as far as dormitories and domestic arrangements are concerned, for the reception of about three hundred and twenty, perhaps three hundred and fifty boys. The three cottages for masters and their families, standing near the school, were finished in the years 1885, 1887, and 1889 respectively. Together they cost about eighteen thousand dollars. Besides the purchases of property already mentioned, several other additions to the estate have been made at different times. The Howe farm of thirty acres was bought in 1875. The two Hall farms, containing together two hundred and seventy-six acres, were purchased in 1885 and 1886. The Goodwin property, with thirty acres, was bought in 1882. The farm-houses on these properties were all repaired and put to use. The saw mill, long known as Fry's, which for many years did much injury by filling up the pond with its refuse, was bought, together with twenty acres of land, in 1881. Two other cottages and about ten acres were added in 1885 and 1886. The entire cost of all these pieces of property, together with improvements and repairs, was about twenty-five thousand dollars. The present land estate owned by the corporation is nearly five hundred and fifty acres. It forms a compact body surrounding the group of buildings on all sides, but extends much more to the south and west of them than to the north or east. There are on this property twenty houses, in which boys, masters, and employés of the school live. Nine other buildings are used for various purposes connected with the instruction and training of the scholars, or with their athletic sports and exercises. There are also a laundry and repair shop, two capacious barns, a large stable with store rooms, ice house, and blacksmith's forge adjoining, and four or five sheds in which farm produce and all sorts of articles are kept. Finally, the old and new chapels complete the list of buildings.

As early as 1875 the need of a new chapel began to be seriously felt. Even before that date the boys had not only filled up the part set apart for them in the founder's chapel, but had gradually occupied a large number of seats appropriated to the general congregation. Each increase in the roll of pupils required that more places should be taken for the school. After a while, at the eleven o'clock morning service, the chapel was uncomfortably crowded. On special occasions it became almost impossible to provide seats for the boys and visitors who were expected to be present. During the four or five years preceding the erection of the new chapel, the old one was almost entirely filled by the boys at the services which they attended. In order to provide for the religious care of the families of masters, of many of the employés, and of the people living near by, two services on Sunday were especially arranged for them in addition to those appointed for the school, and, in this way, two congregations grew up. The year 1880 was marked by the first steps toward raising a fund for a new chapel. There had been much talk about a movement of this kind for a long time. The need became greater from year to year, and each recurring Easter and anniversary brought the matter to the immediate attention of many alumni and friends; but the rector's wife gave the initiative impulse and received the first gifts. She caused boxes to be put in the vestibules, through which the boys and others passed to attend service, with notices stating that they were for contributions to a new chapel. The talks in the rectory parlors, the enthusiasm and interest which gradually sprung up among some of the alumni, masters, and boys, led at last to definite plans and efforts. St. Paul's is under deep and lasting obligations to the Rev. William Stanley Emery for the time, energy, and labor which he devoted to the chapel fund. He had been for seven years in the school as a boy, and had imbibed an ardent affection for the place. "For his brethren and companions' sakes," for the good of the school, he was willing to make the largest sacrifices. He brought forward at the annual meeting of the Alumni Association, in June, 1882, the following resolution:

"*Resolved,* That a committee of five be appointed to take such measures as they shall think advisable to assist in securing a building fund for the new chapel."

The motion was energetically opposed* on various grounds, the principal one urged being that this new project would interfere with the completion of a scholarship which the alumni had begun some years before. At first sight, also, it did seem that to raise forty or fifty thousand dollars was too large an undertaking for an association, most of whose members were quite young men. But Mr. Emery's courage and confidence overcame the doubts and fears of his comrades. His resolution was carried, and the following committee was appointed:

>WILLIAM S. EMERY, Boston,
>P. EVARTS, New York,
>E. D. APPLETON, New York,
>H. MARQUAND, New York,
>H. S. CARTER, New York.

The committee did not consider their duty a nominal one. They proceeded at once to organize and begin their efforts.† In the course of the year one member, Mr. H. Marquand (a son of Mr. Henry G. Marquand, of New York, whose name will always be gratefully remembered at St. Paul's School for many munificent gifts during the past twenty years) was obliged to withdraw for reasons which he could not set aside, and his place was filled by the Rev. George W. Douglass, then one of the assistant ministers of Trinity Church,

---

* See published minutes of this meeting.

† Their first circular was sent out in the November following their appointment.

New York, and now rector of St. John's Church, Washington.

Mr. F. A. Marquand was elected treasurer of the funds to be collected.

During the first year after the appointment of the committee there was some discussion as to how much money should be asked for. Sixty thousand dollars was thought by many persons to be the utmost that ought to be named, nor should all of this amount in their opinion be given to the fabric. Fifteen or twenty thousand dollars ought to be reserved for its endowment, to defray the expense of necessary repairs and of warming and lighting it. But the experience of the committee very early enlarged their hopes and ideas. The best evidence of their indefatigable and successful labors is found in the report they presented to the association at the annual meeting in 1883. The subscriptions they had received up to that date amounted to $51,683; the actual sum paid in was $38,516. In this report they announced their intention to raise if possible $100,000; this amount they thought would be sufficient to build a chapel and provide a fund for its maintenance. At this meeting the alumni felt justified in asking the trustees to appoint a building committee, and it requested that the association might be represented on this committee by two of the members resident at Concord. The following resolution was unanimously carried at this same meeting.

"*Resolved*, That the hearty thanks of the association are hereby given to the members of the Chapel Committee, and especially to Mr. W. S. Emery, for the unwearied and successful efforts which have been made in raising a fund for the new chapel."

The corporation, at its annual meeting, held June 19, 1883, in accordance with the request of the alumni, appointed the following building committee: The rector and vice-rector, Dr. Samuel Eliot, trustees, and the Rev. John Hargate, Mr. James C. Knox, Dr. Henry S. Carter, and the Rev. W. Stanley Emery, alumni.

Sketches for a new chapel were obtained from Mr. Henry Vaughan, of Boston. The designs presented by this gentleman were finally approved, and he was appointed architect. Mr. Vaughan was a pupil of the celebrated English architects, Messrs. Bodley and Garner, and had been thoroughly trained for his profession. He has proved by his work that he has excellent taste, imaginative and inventive faculties of no mean order, besides tact and judgment. The building committee made a happy selection in choosing Mr. Vaughan to be the architect of the new chapel.

As soon as the project was fairly started, the alumni and friends of the school aided it in the most active and generous way. The Chapel Fund Committee not only devoted themselves to their work heartily, but they inspired a large number of persons with warm interest. By May, 1885, the fund had grown to over $80,000, and at the annual meeting of the Association held May 27, 1886, the total amount reported was $101,344.08. Of this sum, $86,034.08 was cash in the hands of the treasurer. The remainder, $15,310, consisted of subscriptions which would certainly be paid in, with the exception of perhaps $1,000. A contract was made during the spring of 1886 for the erection of the fabric (without tower, heating or lighting arrangements, or furniture of any sort) for $73,000. The foundation was put in during the summer and the corner-stone was laid by Dr. Shattuck, in the presence of a large assembly, on September 21st, St. Matthew's day, 1886.

The subscription list contained several large and generous contributions. Mr. Henry G. Marquand and his family gave $15,000; Mrs. M. B. Stevens, of Hoboken, New Jersey, and her sons, $22,500; Mrs. Charles Wheeler, of Philadelphia, $5,500; Mrs. A. M. Hoyt, of New York, $2,500. There was a goodly number of subscriptions of $1,000, many of $500, $250, and $100. The complete list of subscribers to the fund is a most gratifying evidence of a strong regard for the school on the part of the alumni, and of a truly generous appreciation on the part of their parents and friends. From many of the alumni no contributions were received, not from want of good will, but because they were young men whose incomes were small, or because other more imperative obligations prevented them. There was a remarkable display of kind feeling and loyal attachment called forth by the chapel fund, and to those most deeply concerned for the welfare of the school it was a happy omen for the future. The fund raised by the alumni, after $25,000 had been set apart from it as an endowment for the maintenance of the chapel, was simply sufficient to pay the price named in the contract and the architect's fees. But the interior, if finished according to Mr.

Vaughan's designs, required a large additional outlay. Toward this object there have been several costly gifts presented and certain special funds provided. The altar was given by the family of one of the masters, in commemoration of a name very sacred and dear to them. The bishop's seat, a richly carved chair, was the gift of another master, a generous and sincere friend of St. Paul's.[*] The font with its oak cover was given by Mrs. Dr. Coit and her sister, Miss E. B. Wheeler, of Philadelphia. The pulpit was presented by the sixth form of 1888. The lectern, credence, and faldstool were provided either by special gift or by the rector. The stalls with their canopies, the benches, the screen and gallery separating choir and ante-chapel were paid for from a new fund raised directly for this object. A happy suggestion, made by one of the masters, to appropriate each stall to some one who had been connected with the school, either as trustee, master, or boy, was at once warmly approved. The fact that the name of the person to whom the stall was assigned would be placed on it, made a lively appeal to the sentiment and affection of many. They took pleasure in the thought that their names would be permanently associated with the beautiful chapel and thus preserved at the school. The applications for stalls were many more than could be granted. The subscription for a stall was $125, if it was situated in the chancel, and $100, if it was in the choir. The entire eighty-six stalls were very speedily taken up. The

---

[*] Mr. James M. Lamberton

trustees added to the sum obtained in this way the remainder of Dr. Shattuck's gift to the old chapel. This sum, amounting to $1,922, was now, with his permission, devoted to the new. Two or three contributions of sums between $100 and $500 were also received, and the rector completed the amount necessary. The total cost of stalls, gallery, and screen was $12,330. There were other outlays for the curtain behind the altar, the steam-heating and gas fixtures, the hassocks, rugs, and chairs, which amounted in all to nearly $4,500, and were paid by the rector. The organ was procured, as has already been stated, through the indefatigable efforts of Mr. James C. Knox. The contributions came chiefly from friends of the lamented Mr. A. M. Swift, and they were accompanied in many cases by letters conveying warm and affectionate tributes to his memory. The total cost of the organ was $8,676.81.

Three stained-glass windows have been put in, all of them the work of Messrs. Clayton and Bell, of London. Four more have been given, two of which will soon be set in their places.* The windows already provided are very beautiful; good judges say that they are among the finest and most artistic in execution on this side of the Atlantic.

---

* The two windows here spoken of are now (March, 1891), set up. They have come from the same makers as the others and are very handsome and appropriate. One of them is the gift of the fifth form of 1889; the other has been placed as a memorial to their mother, by the sons of Mr. George E. Mumford, of Rochester, New York, members of the school during the last fifteen years.

The Paine window in the chancel, a memorial to their deceased mother given by two members of the school, is remarkably good. The lovely west window has been placed in commemoration of Mrs. Dr. Coit by her family. The remaining one of the three was given by the fifth form of 1888. These windows together with the pulpit, lectern, and other articles of furniture cost about $11,000. Altogether there has been expended on the new chapel, $117,740.43, in addition to the $25,000 provided for endowment. Twenty-five hundred dollars have also been paid out for grading, for laying drains, and for sundry like matters. The entire sum devoted thus far to the new chapel and its maintenance has been $142,500. There are still many things to be done before the building can properly be called finished. The tower, the reredos, the cloister connecting school-house and chapel, nine stained-glass windows (of which, three are the large ones in the chancel, and one is the great window over the porch), bells, clock, and additional chancel furniture make up a list of objects which will all be given in good time. The building is so noble and beautiful that the alumni and friends who have taken such delight in bringing it to its present state may confidently be relied upon for its proper completion.

The new chapel was consecrated on June 5, 1888. Two bishops, forty clergy, and a great company of trustees, alumni, and friends of the school were present. The Rt. Rev. Henry C. Potter, Bishop of New York, was the preacher, and he spoke with a wisdom and sympathy that can never be forgotten by those who listened to him. The sermon was a noble plea for religious education. The aims and results of the work at St. Paul's have never been stated with more insight and appreciation than on this occasion. The following eloquent passage may serve as an illustration:

"'Humility, dependence, humanity, love.' My brethren, these are the things that have been pre-eminently taught here. The record of this school is not devoid of honors won by its sons on many fields of endeavor and in many halls of learning. The standard of its scholarship, as illustrated in the standing of its pupils, is such as any mother might point to with just pride. But its pre-eminent distinction has been that it has taught its children faith and reverence and the eternal sanctity of duty. And these things it has taught not alone in the class-room, by text-book, through the impressive lessons of history, but most of all in St. Paul's Chapel. The daily prayers, the weekly sacraments, the well remembered sermons, the Sunday afternoon Bible lessons—these have been powers that have taught Christ's presence in his Church and Christ's message to his children in a language never to be forgotten. Once and again and again—I know it from testimonies which might well be brought here to help to hallow by their inspiring memories this holy and beautiful house—has some young life, struggling in the meshes of strong temptation, torn by doubt or smitten by a sense of its sin, heard from yonder altar or yonder pulpit words of hope and pardon, a message of life-giving love and courage. Once, and again and again, have young feet, turning thither tardily and reluctantly, found themselves, like Jacob at Peniel, halted on their earthly way, and called to climb the gleaming ladder ascending to the skies. Ah! my young brothers, alumni of this school, am I not telling the story of some of you as I speak these words? As you come back here to-day, to join with us in giving this sanctuary—your gift—to God, do not your hearts turn to the dear old chapel—the hallowed place which those who have come after you have found 'too strait'—with tender and inextinguishable devotion? The convictions that are deepest in your lives to-day, the faith that, when the world scoffs, yet lives and glows within you, the reverence for goodness, the love of nobleness—tell me, are not these things linked in your memories with lessons that you learned here, lessons which you will never forget?"

The consecration had been looked forward to as a great and joyful event. And so it was in truth; but the day has also very sad memories associated with it. The two persons most deeply interested in the new chapel, and for whom its completion signified most, were at the time both grievously afflicted. The rector had met with a serious accident (compound fracture of a leg) early in the winter, and, after a long and painful confinement, had just begun to move about with the aid of crutches. His wife, after months of gradual decline, had reached those stages of feebleness and suffering which precede by only a short interval the close of life. It seemed strange indeed not to hear Dr. Coit's voice in the service, nor to meet Mrs. Coit and himself in the accustomed ways during the festivities of that day and of the anniversary which immediately followed. All were thankful that both were able at least to be present at the consecration. This was one of the three occasions in which Mrs. Coit came inside the new chapel after its completion. She was permitted to see the fulfilment of a project very dear to her, one which owed its beginning to her efforts. But within three months after the consecration her beautiful and most useful life was ended.

The tower, which it is hoped will be built in the next two years, has been selected as an appropriate memorial to one to whom St. Paul's is most deeply indebted, whose loving and wise heart, self-sacrifice, and devotion co-operating with the special gifts of her husband exerted the largest and best influence in moulding and fashioning its life and spirit.

Mary Bowman Wheeler, third daughter and fourth child of Charles Wheeler and Eliza his wife, was born in Philadelphia, which continued to be her home until her marriage. Her father was a learned and respected lawyer, a member of the Philadelphia bar, a man of high principles, and a devout Churchman. Her mother, Eliza Bowman, was the sister of Dr. Bowman, Assistant Bishop of Pennsylvania, Colonel Bowman, Commandant at West Point, and Mrs. May, wife of the Rev. Dr. May, of the Alexandria Seminary. The father of Eliza Bowman, Captain Samuel Bowman, fought in the War of Independence, knew Washington, was a friend of Alexander Hamilton, and attended Major André to execution. The wife of Captain Bowman was Eleanor Leslie, daughter of William Leslie, an Englishman, and his wife, Eleanor Stewart, a member of the Stewart family of County Tyrone, which in the persons of Lord Castle Stewart and Captain Andrew Stewart received grants of property in the north of Ireland from King James I. Mary Bowman Wheeler was married in the Church of the Epiphany, Philadelphia, March 27, 1856, to the Rev. Henry Augustus Coit. Eight days later she arrived at her new home in Concord. Here for thirty-two years her life was devoted not only to the discharge of the duties which came upon her as wife and mother, but also to incessant labors in behalf of the school, the community which surrounded it, and the manifold charities which appealed to her sympathy and pity. Until 1870, when the Upper School was built, Mrs. Coit had the entire management of household matters. There was of course a housekeeper or matron to assist, but the comfort and economy with which the school was carried on were due to the unwearied attention and wise control of the rector's wife. In those years when the boys lived under the same roof with her she was constantly planning for their happiness and improvement. If they were sick, she looked after them as their own mothers would have done. If they were downhearted or in trouble, she had the art of winning their confidence and giving them the right sort of sympathy and help. If they were reckless or troublesome, they had in her a friend who did not despair of their coming to a better mind, and who was eager to welcome and foster every token of improvement. As long as the school was quite small, it was

SUBSEQUENT HISTORY.

truly like a home, and the joys and troubles of every member were the common concern of all, and for three or four years even the birthdays which fell in term time were duly celebrated. In the front parlor and library were gathered evening after evening groups of boys, playing games, listening to stories delightfully read, singing, talking, or engaged in such tasks as getting up tablets, Easter eggs, and the like. Mrs. Coit sat in the midst, as merry as any of the party, contributing to the pleasure of all, but at the same time devoting special attention to those who were shy or neglected by their companions. Her refinement was so real and her manners so gracious that the boys in her presence were never ill-behaved. Many of them learned from her how to be unselfish and to care for others. The charm exerted by her lovely disposition, her bright and pleasant talk, her sympathetic and kindly ways, drew out the best traits and feelings of the young company. Visitors in those days, even as now, were coming and going continually. The care of their entertainment fell chiefly upon Mrs. Coit, and it was her delight not only to make the guests comfortable, but also to render their visit pleasant in every way. Hospitality at that time, when the house was crowded and all the arrangements were on a contracted scale, cost personal attention and careful planning. At Thanksgiving, Easter, anniversary, and the other festal days of the year, the greatest pains were taken to provide excellent and bountiful repasts, and although Mrs. Coit had many exacting social duties as wife of the rector, yet she found time, how or when it is hard to say, in which to superintend the necessary preparations. In fact, there was hardly any part of the school life which did not feel her influence or which did not benefit in some way or other, directly or indirectly, from her interest, her sympathy, or her actual efforts. After the removal of Dr. Coit and his family to the rectory, in 1872, his wife was apparently relieved from many of the domestic cares, the burden of which she had hitherto cheerfully borne. But in reality the only change that took place was in the increased number of the demands made upon her and the more difficult character of them. Upper School, Lower School, and School now looked to her for counsel and direction in the management of domestic affairs. Her large experience and unselfish sympathy had constant appeals made to them. Her tact and patience solved many a burning question, rectified mistakes, pacified unruly servants, and put new heart into the desponding. How many hours of her much occupied time were given without grudging to masters seeking sympathy or help in their projects, to boys with plans for themselves or their clubs, or arranging for visits from their friends, to matrons perplexed by some *contretemps* or novel incident, to servants dissatisfied and aggrieved. The rectory was the scene of most gracious and liberal hospitality. There were very few days when the family sat down to dinner without guests. Convalescing and homesick boys were invited there to stay until recovery was complete. A constant succession of parties of boys were coming, either to dine or to take tea or to evening entertainments. Trustees, lecturers, examiners, distinguished strangers, bishops, and clergy made up each year a long list of guests. But Mrs. Coit's cares and interests were not confined to the school and its affairs. The Orphans' Home was really organized by her, and her energetic interest was its chief support until her death. Wherever there was sickness, sorrow, or need in the neighborhood, thither she would go to minister and to help. She gained the confidence and affectionate respect of the entire community which surrounds the school. People learned to trust her goodness and sincerity; to seek her counsel and to rely on it. They found out that she went in and out among them moved by no selfish or vulgar motive, but led by love unfeigned and out of a pure heart. She taught in the Sunday school for years, and the children delighted to come to her classes. They became objects of her special care and were not lost sight of as they increased in age. And her compassionate nature did not suffer her to be indifferent to the great church societies. She was always doing something for domestic or foreign missions, for the negroes, for destitute families or individuals throughout the country. No appeal was ever made to her which she disregarded. There seemed to be no limits to her sympathies and efforts for those in "trouble, sorrow, need, sickness, or any other adversity." What a blessing to a great school to have such a woman living in it, sharing in its management, and devoted to its interests! What a precious and inspiring memory has she left to be honored and revered! Among those specially to be commemorated as benefactors, as having by gifts and deeds, by wisdom and zeal, by love and patience, assisted to rear St. Paul's School, no name is more worthy than that of Mrs. Mary Bowman Coit.

The designs for the tower of the new chapel give room for a peal of bells. These would not displace the bells of the old chapel and school-house now in use, and the set would only be rung together on Sundays and festive occasions, or in honor of some great benefaction, or to celebrate the marriage of a Concordian. But the occasions would be sufficiently numerous, and the mere naming of these few uses shows how much pleasure and how many delightful associations would come from such a peal.

And here seems to be the fitting place to give a brief account of the association which has done so important and good a work for St. Paul's. It was formed in 1872 with the purpose of helping, in all ways possible, the great objects of the school. At this time, the number of alumni being small and the oldest among them only young men just beginning their careers, nothing more was attempted than the recognition of a tie binding them together and of a purpose to do something when they had the power and opportunity. But they early took three practical steps to make the association more than a mere name. First, they determined to have an annual public meeting at the anniversary, with addresses by speakers selected from among their own number; second, at the request of the rector they appointed committees to attend and assist in the examinations; and, third, they resolved to raise ten thousand dollars to found a scholarship to be called,

SUBSEQUENT HISTORY.

in token of their love and regard for the rector, the Coit scholarship. After ten years' existence the association felt strong enough to begin the collection of the new chapel fund. The scholarship fund has been completed and paid over to the treasurer of the corporation. The history of the chapel fund has already been told. Probably the association will take up soon an endowment scheme; of such a movement there is very great need. The educational appliances and institutions now gathered at St. Paul's can not be secured for future generations, nor can the fruits of the many munificent gifts and the results of the years of devoted labor and sacrifice be preserved and handed on without sufficient endowment. The permanent funds of the school amount at present to $128,348.97. Of these funds the part appropriated to scholarships or prizes is $49,880.27, distributed as follows:

Two founder's scholarships	$17,281 42
One Coit scholarship	11,482 57
Stebbins and Winchester (named thus in memory of two deceased alumni) scholarship	897 44
One Clark scholarship (founded by Christ Church, Philadelphia)	8,591 40
Two Ferguson scholarships (income $250 each; founded as prizes by the Rev. Prof. Ferguson, of Trinity College)	10,194 52
One John Lord Day scholarship (founded in memory of a deceased alumnus by his parents)	1,309 56
English composition prize fund (founded by the sixth form of 1873)	123 36

The remaining permanent funds, amounting to $78,468.70, are apportioned as follows:

Repair fund (founded by Dr. Shattuck)	$5,583.84
Swift endowment (given by the late John H. Swift, a trustee)	12,580.10
Permanent endowment (derived from the entrance fees) .	29,229.76
Chapel maintenance fund (founded by the Alumni Association	26,075.00
Noyes fund (bequest of Samuel W. Noyes) . . .	5,000.00

The income from the permanent funds available for school purposes does not at present exceed four thousand dollars. It is obvious that a capital yielding five or six times greater income than this would not be more than sufficient for the security of so large a work as that at St. Paul's has become. A considerable part of the present endowment has been derived from careful financial management. The incomes of nearly all the different funds have generally been added to the funds themselves instead of being used in carrying on the school. For example, the total income from the permanent funds for the year ending June 1, 1890, was $5,831.33; of this amount there was handed over $2,149.89 on account of the Coit, Clark, and founder's scholarships, the English composition prize fund, and the chapel maintenance fund. A small sum ($146.66) was appropriated to certain minor expenses. The remainder was added to the various funds. Persons ask, Why is an endowment of four or five hundred thousand dollars necessary? Does not the annual income from the charges for the boys more than pay

SUBSEQUENT HISTORY. 117

all expenses? It is true that the annual income has not only borne all expenses, but that from it, as a rule, a considerable sum has been saved every year for gratuitous education, for buildings, or for purchase of land. But the work of the school has always been, to a certain extent, crippled by the curtailments which these savings and the effort to make them have involved. In fact, the whole annual income ought to be devoted to the current expenses necessary for carrying on the work to the best advantage, and the time is speedily approaching when it will barely meet the actual needs of the school for this purpose. The preceding pages have shown what a variety of apparatus and what numerous agencies are employed in a great school which must provide not only tuition, but comfortable lodging and suitable maintenance for more than three hundred boys. A first-rate school is a costly establishment, and in proportion to the completeness and perfection of its equipment do its annual charges, unless very high, fail to bring in an income sufficient to meet all its manifold expenses.* Experienced and competent masters can not

---

* The annual charges for tuition and residence from 1856 to 1865 were three hundred dollars. Few or no extras were in those years put on the bills. From 1865 to 1867 the price was advanced to four hundred dollars. In 1867 the present charges were adopted. But these advances were made with great reluctance and under the pressure of necessity. Many friends of the school think that the time has arrived for an increase of the annual charges to six hundred dollars. If a sufficient endowment is long delayed, perhaps such an increase may become necessary, for the expenses of carrying on the school are steadily growing in proportion as the various apparatus

be secured and retained except when paid good salaries, and when they know, at the same time, that they may count upon the continuance of their engagements as long as their powers and usefulness last. The cold New England winter requires large outlays to remove snow from roofs and walks, to keep the living and working rooms well warmed and ventilated, and to provide healthy occupations and amusements during the long months when the snow lies deep on the ground. A tradition of hospitality has come down which it would be a serious loss to infringe, and yet it can easily be seen that it is an increasingly heavy item in the expense account. There has always prevailed a generous way of treating the boys and a marked absence of scrimping or of any wish or effort to make money out of them. It would change the spirit of St. Paul's very much, if, under the pressure of a rigid economy, a more detailed and exact system of charges was adopted. A sufficient endowment would keep the school charges at or near their present moderate figure. It would leave the annual income free to go toward providing for the ordinary expenses of the year, and it would supplement any deficiency. In case of serious loss or misfortune it would greatly diminish the ill results, and, in many instances, would enable the school to recover quickly from disaster.

---

and conveniences are augmented or enlarged. But the intention and desire of the trustees is to keep the present charges unaltered, if possible. The idea has been to make the school an institution which gives more than it receives. In 1878 an entrance fee of twenty-five dollars was established by the trustees, and the proceeds devoted to a permanent endowment fund.

It would furnish the corporation with the power to make desirable improvements, to extend and enlarge the work, to add to the apparatus for education without appealing or waiting for assistance from others.

Endowment should be distributed under various heads. There should be a repair and insurance fund, a salary fund, a general fund applicable to any special need, a library and apparatus fund, a choir fund, a gymnasium fund. At present there are six scholarships, three of them of the full value of ten thousand dollars each. There should be at least twenty or twenty-five of full value. Such scholarships would keep up, even in disastrous times, the continuous life of the school with its traditions and customs; they would also bring in a most desirable element, namely, boys with a purpose and motive to work and do their best; and they would often afford the opportunities of a good education to those eminently worthy of it, who, without such aid, would be debarred from it.

The school greatly needs funds devoted, as the Ferguson scholarships are, to raising the standard in the chief studies and to stimulating better efforts for accurate knowledge of the different subjects pursued. Mr. Ferguson, by his wise and generous action, has done St. Paul's a great and lasting benefit. The two scholarships founded by him are among the chief honors of the school. They are open by competition to boys in the third and fourth forms. A third-former, to get the prize, must pass satisfactorily written examinations on the Greek, Latin, and Algebra which have been studied during the year. A boy in the fourth form must fulfil similar conditions in order to win one of these scholarships. The two who come out best in the examinations are announced by name during a public meeting at the end of the session as the Ferguson scholars for the ensuing year, and receive the cordial and lively plaudits of their companions and friends. The English composition prize fund, established by an enthusiastic sixth form in 1873, is the only fund for the encouragement of a special study which has yet been given.* But there ought to be French and German scholarships, drawing and handwriting, reading and spelling prizes. The study of Latin and Greek would be helped by scholarships granted for successful examinations on portions of specified authors or in prose composition. For excellence in some one of the different

---

* Prizes have lately been founded by a bequest of the Rev. Thomas G. Valpey, for many years a master A piece of real estate, probably having a value of about three thousand dollars, and situated adjoining the school domain, was left for this purpose under certain conditions. The property is to be divided into lots, which are to be sold at public auction, and three fourths of the proceeds of the sale are to be invested as a permanent prize fund. These prizes are to be named from the donor. Another former master, Mr Charles A. Mitchell, now residing in Cleveland, Ohio, in token of his attachment to St. Paul's (an attachment which is warmly reciprocated by his former associates as well as by the boys who had the benefit of his excellent teaching and unwearied kindness), has signified his intention of founding a Greek prize. His purpose is to provide a fund, the income of which shall supply a gold medal, to be given to that boy of the fifth or sixth form who, at the end of the session, passes the best examination in some specified reading in Greek.

subjects in mathematics pursued at the school scholarships could be offered with great advantage to those studies. A capital of eight hundred dollars would yield income sufficient to provide first and second prizes in a given subject; three hundred or four hundred dollars would yield sufficient income for a single prize. The statutes of the corporation stipulate that any prize or scholarship fund shall be named after its donor, if it is so desired, and that any conditions attached by him to the gift shall be observed, if not conflicting with the rules and customs of the school.

The subject of endowment has already been seriously considered by several prominent alumni. In 1882 Mr. George Harrison Fisher, of Philadelphia, now a trustee, prepared for the Alumni Association *A Plan to create a Trust for the Supply of a Fund for an Endowment at St. Paul's School.* This plan, however, only embraces endowment by scholarships. It is drawn very skilfully by a trained lawyer, and contains the main provisions which ought to be adopted for the protection and administration of such funds. They are these:

1. The fund must be held by the corporation in trust for the objects proposed.

2. Investments must be made only in certain specified classes of securities.

3. The capital funds must under no circumstances be expended or diverted from the trust objects.

4. The income so far as the same extends must be devoted toward the maintenance of scholars.

The first three provisions apply to all classes of endowment funds.

Before passing from the account of the Alumni Association, it surely will not be considered invidious to name specially three or four out of that large body of cordial and generous friends of St. Paul s. The services of the Rev. E. M. Parker to the association, as its secretary, have been invaluable. His duties have entailed great labors, but they have been labors of love. The roll of the alumni lately prepared by him contains information interesting to every Concordian, and this information is, moreover, remarkably accurate. The Alumni Annual is also due to Mr. Parker's efforts. It never fails to be welcomed wherever it is sent and to arouse kindly memories in all its readers.

To another alumnus, Major Charles H. Whipple, U. S. A., the school has been greatly indebted for giving annually since 1874 a gold medal to the boy passing the best written examination on an assigned theme in English literature. A play of Shakespeare has generally been selected as the subject. On nine occasions the celebrated Shakespearean scholar, the Rev. Henry N. Hudson, set the question paper, made the decisions, and conferred the prizes. He always gave a short address to the boys when announcing the results of the examination, and he won their hearts and minds to his way of thinking entirely. He talked to them about literature, particular books and authors, in language within the comprehension of the youngest—vigorous, racy, often full of poetical thoughts, and always holding the attention of his hearers. He came to be regarded by the boys in the light of a friend. His visits were looked forward to with pleasure, and his lectures, talks, and sermons greatly enjoyed. He was himself an enthusiastic admirer of the school, and his warmth of regard for it and for all its interests greatly enhanced the pleasure of his visits.

Mr. Henry Marquand, Jr., is another alumnus whose generous interest in the library must not be forgotten. There are many valuable books on the shelves which are his gifts. His brother, the lamented Frederick Alexander Marquand, was treasurer of the chapel fund until his death in 1886. The alumni testified their appreciation of his valuable services and lovely character by placing a stall to his memory in the chancel of the new chapel. After Mr. Marquand's death, Mr. Henry Parish, Jr., of New York city discharged the duties of treasurer in compliance with the request of the Chapel Fund Committee. The labor and trouble which the office involved were cheerfully given by Mr. Parish, and his services were gratefully appreciated by the trustees and the rector.

Mr. Thomas Chew Lewis, an alumnus and devoted friend of St. Paul's, died in 1882, leaving to the school as a token of affectionate remembrance a bequest of five thousand dollars. This sum was appropriated by the trustees to the purchase of the Goodwin property. The old house, repaired and enlarged, is used as the residence of a master, and in accordance with a vote of the corporation is called "the Lewis Cottage."

At the annual meeting of the trustees in 1889, the announcement was made that Mr. Samuel W. Noyes, of Providence, lately deceased, had bequeathed to the school, in memory of his son, Frederick W. Noyes, formerly a pupil at St. Paul's, the sum of five thousand dollars, as a token of his son's faithful and affectionate regard. This bequest has been set apart as a special fund, to be known as the Noyes Fund, and to constitute a part of the endowment.

Many testimonials of their regard and affection have been given by different alumni. The handsome stained-glass window in the common room of the school was presented by the Rev. George W. Lay and Mr. Charles E. Pellew, now an assistant professor in the School of Mines, New York city. The beautiful cross standing on the re-table of the new chapel was the gift of Mr. Lloyd Saltus. These are named as examples of what has been done. One alumnus, Mr. Robert L. Stevens, contributed to the chapel fund the munificent sum of ten thousand dollars. His brother, Mr. Richard Stevens, has lately made the generous subscription of two thousand dollars toward the new Lower School. It would be difficult now to make a complete list of all the tokens of interest and good will which St. Paul's has received from devoted and loyal alumni.* Nothing is more evident

---

* The following list of challenge cups, cricket belts, and medals presented by the association or by old Concordians gives an idea of the sympathy and interest of the alumni in the sports and games and their earnest desire to keep them up to a high standard of excellence:

The Alumni Cricket Cup, offered by the association in 1872. The Ingersoll Cup, given by S. Warren Ingersoll, of Philadelphia, in 1876. The

SUBSEQUENT HISTORY.

than that her sons are proud of their old school, anxious for her honor and success, and glad to help in her advancement.

It is time to revert to two bodies on whom the prosperity and success of St. Paul's have largely depended—the corporation, and the rector and masters. Of the original corporators all are now dead but one, the Right Rev. Bishop Southgate, who resigned in 1860. The successive deaths of Messrs. Otis,

---

Pellew Cup, given by Charles Earnest Pellew, of New York, in 1880. The Brooks Cup, given by Lawrence Brooks, of Boston, in 1885. The Mackay-Smith Cup, given by the Rev. Dr. Alexander Mackay-Smith, of New York, in 1887. The Boudinot Cricket Belt, presented by E. Boudinot, of Philadelphia, in 1872. The Hayden Cricket Belt, presented by William Langdon Hayden, of Columbus, Ohio, in 1890.

The Challenge Cup for the senior half mile, given by Augustus Peabody Gardner, of Boston. The Challenge Cup for the hurdle race, given by Russell F. Robbins, of Brooklyn. The Challenge Cup for the senior two hundred and twenty yards dash, given by Robert L. Stevens, of Hoboken, N. J. The Harvard Challenge Cup for all track athletics, given by the alumni of St. Paul's School in Harvard University, in 1890. A challenge cup, for the senior hundred yards, given by Howard Van Rensselaer, of Albany, and George Westervelt, of New Brighton, Staten Island. The Challenge Cup for the one mile walk, given by the Rev. Prescott Evarts, of New York. The Curtis Challenge Cup, given by F. Kingsbury Curtis, of New York The medal for the senior quarter mile, presented by Edward Clarkson Potter, of New York. The Second Crew Challenge Cup, given by Charles A. Brayton, of Cleveland, Ohio. The First Crew Challenge Cup was given in 1890 by Mr. Alfred E Harrison, of Philadelphia, a warm friend of St. Paul's, in the name of his son, now a pupil in the school. A medal for the single scull race, given by the Rev James P. Conover and John D. Cheever, of New York. The cups are all of solid silver, and are very handsome.

Coale, and Parker, all warmly interested trustees, during the first seven years of the school's existence, were deeply lamented. A beautiful stained-glass window over the altar of the old chapel commemorates the valued services and high character of Mr. Otis. A stall in the chancel of the new chapel bears the honored name of Henry M. Parker, trustee, father of two sons—both alumni of St. Paul's and both devoted friends of the place.

There have been twenty-six members of the board of trustees since the act of incorporation was passed; six of these, for good reasons, resigned their positions after different terms of service. Twelve—including five of those who have resigned—have died. The rector has been a trustee thirty-three years. Dr. Samuel Eliot, of Boston, has belonged to the corporation since 1858. His services to the school have been numberless. His high standard of scholarship and acquirement, his broad and liberal culture, his exquisite taste in literature and full knowledge of its various departments have enabled him, as examiner, lecturer, awarder of prizes, and visitor, to render the wisest assistance in the intellectual work of the school. His example of devout piety, of voluntary sacrifices for the good of city and State, and of active exertion for every worthy cause, has been full of helpful influences to those who have had the privilege of knowing him as a counsellor and friend. Mr. John H. Swift, of New York, was a trustee from 1864 to 1879, when ill-health compelled him to resign; but the school had no more enthusiastic friend than Mr. Swift during his days of health. He was unwearied in kind acts, and ready to give liberal help to any project for the good of St. Paul's. The endowment would now be a nearly accomplished fact had certain investments which he made of the great bulk of his fortune turned out as prosperous as he had expected. His latter days were clouded by business anxieties and disappointments, and his end was very sad ; but every remembrance of him at St. Paul's is pleasant. The Swift foundation, now amounting to over thirteen thousand dollars, is a lasting proof of his regard and appreciation. One would like to dwell upon the valued services of Mr. Richard H. Dana, the distinguished lawyer and author. He was the warm friend of the rector, a sagacious adviser, and a welcome and helpful visitor. His son, bearing the same name, seems to have inherited without diminution his father's love of country and zeal for righteousness and truth. As an alumnus he has been among the foremost in promoting the interests of St. Paul's. Bishop Chase was a wise and faithful trustee, and during the early years of the school his advice was of very great service. On his death Bishop Niles, whose learning and piety commend him to all who know him, was elected to fill the vacancy, and his presence at examinations, at the public exercises, and at the meetings of the board, has been very constant and helpful. Special mention ought to be made of the valuable portraits of the founder and the rector by the celebrated artist Healey, presented to the school by Mr. William C. Sheldon, a trustee. This gift is only one of many tokens of regard which St. Paul's has received from Mr. Sheldon. But to do justice to the faithful and kindly services of the different trustees would require many pages; each has benefited St. Paul's by special offices, and all, in various ways, have aided the work. Two characteristic features have distinguished the policy of the trustees. One is the hearty confidence and support which they have uniformly given to the rector of the school. Having quickly seen that Dr. Coit was a man of remarkable fitness for his office, with a genius for the government and training of boys; that he had scholarship, literary culture, power to teach and inspire others, was unselfish, self-sacrificing, of sound judgment, and tied to no fancies or theories, they gave him full scope to fashion and conduct the school according to his own plans. They left him free to choose his assistants and fellow-workers, to order the routine of occupations, studies, and recreation as he might think best, and they hampered him as little as possible in the disposition of the income. Individual trustees have often doubtless differed with the rector as to the wisdom of certain outlays of money, or as to the actual benefit of certain features of the discipline or general policy of the school. But virtually the board has been unanimous in their approval and support of the rector, and they have shown the truest wisdom in the freedom of action which they have given him. They have been more than satisfied with the success of his administration financially and with the moral and intellectual condition of the school under his government. They have had, therefore, no reason or wish to disturb the relation and conditions which produce the results they witness.*

---

* In 1867 Dr. Coit was elected President of Trinity College, to fill the place of the Rev. Dr. Kerfoot, who had been made Bishop of Pittsburg. Although the acceptance of the office was pressed upon him by bishops and many influential persons, yet, happily for St. Paul's School, Dr. Coit declined the honor, and preferred to go on with the work which he had undertaken. In 1871 Dr. Coit was elected to the presidency of Hobart College, and strong inducements were offered to lead him to a favorable consideration of the invitation; but the same motives and reasons which determined the answer in 1867 determined it four years later. The following letter, addressed to Dr Coit by the trustees shortly after he had declined the presidency of Hobart College, shows very clearly in what high estimation he was held by the corporation, how warmly they appreciated his past work, and how strong was their confidence in him:

August 18, 1871

REVEREND AND DEAR SIR: A formal vote, entered on the records, will not satisfy the desire we all feel to assure you of our gratitude, and of our deep sense of the disinterested character of the course you have lately taken as to St Paul's School, and of the great effect we believe it will have on the school, and on those great interests beyond the school which you and we have alike at heart.

We therefore desire to address you personally as well as in our official capacity as trustees.

We wish you to know that we understand that the presidency of Hobart College, offered to you in the most flattering and attractive manner, presented many inducements to leave your present position, but we rejoice to know that you see in St. Paul's School something to warrant the sacrifice you have made, and we hope that you may find a reward in its prosperity and in the good you may do through it to the Church and country.

On our part, we assure you that we, along with all the friends of the school, recognize an obligation to do our best to see that your situation is made as favorable as possible for the application of your powers and influence to

A second noticeable fact in the history of the corporation has been the few changes in the board during thirty-five years. Only four new members have joined the corporation in the last twenty-five years.

Mr. Charles P. Gardiner has been a member since 1866. He was elected treasurer in 1867, in room of Hon. Josiah Minot, of Concord, who for several years had taken admirable care of the sums given for building and of the permanent funds. The school is under lasting obligations to Mr. Gardiner for his excellent management of its funds.

Mr. Edward Newton Perkins joined the board in 1862. He has been present at all the annual meetings since that date with the exception of four. He has rarely failed, in company with the founder and Dr. Eliot, to visit the school at the spring examinations, and in the closing days of the

---

the highest education of youth, and to the firm establishment of St. Paul's School as a permanent public institution for the whole country

The advance in the requirements for entering the great universities demands a corresponding advance in the character of our preparatory schools. It will be to a great extent in those schools hereafter that the character and intellectual habits of our educated youth will be formed and the foundations of scholarship laid. And we trust that the history of St Paul's School in the future will justify your decision in its favor to your own mind, and to all who have an interest in the appropriate employment of acquirements and influence like yours.

Accept, dear sir, our truest wishes for your health and happiness, and believe us to be, with deep respect,

Faithfully yours,

WILLIAM W. NILES,   H A. NEELY,
I. G. HUBBARD,   J H. COIT,
S. ELIOT,   R. H. DANA, Jr.,
JACOB CARTER,   E. N. PERKINS.
C P. GARDINER,

The Rev Henry A Coit, D. D.,
Rector of St. Paul's School.

SUBSEQUENT HISTORY. 131

session he has generally been present and taken his part in the various exercises. It need hardly be added that his kindly interest and gracious courtesy have been warmly appreciated.

Two of the alumni are now trustees, and the vacancies which hereafter may occur will probably be filled by alumni, whenever suitable men are found willing to undertake the duties. But the slow changing of the body of trustees has been thus far a marked benefit. The school has in the course of years become to the trustees an object of deep interest and regard. Its reverses, its successes, its steady growth and expansion, are to them matters of real concern and excite their lively sympathy. It is this personal acquaintance with the events of each year's history, this direct touch of the life of the great school, which sympathy with it and caring for it give, that has enabled the trustees to aid so judiciously the work carried on at St. Paul's.

Since the opening of the school in 1856, the lists of masters published annually in the Statement have contained in all seventy-nine different names. In this roll of names five *

---

* G. W. D. Copeland, was a master from 1858 to 1860. He died in 1864.

John T. Wheeler was Latin master from 1860 to 1873. He died of consumption at St Luke's Hospital in the fall of 1873 Mr. Wheeler was a man of high principles, a brilliant scholar, and able teacher, and his loss was deeply felt and regretted.

The Rev. Abel A. Kerfoot was the son of Bishop Kerfoot, of Pittsburg. Owing to ill health, he was obliged to resign his mastership after a residence of only one year and a half, in 1863 and part of 1864. But in this short time he won the esteem of his associates and of the boys, by his conscientious discharge of duty and by many lovely traits. He died in are to be lamented as deceased, and of these five, three were connected with the school for periods exceeding ten years. No master has ever died at St. Paul's; very few have had any serious illness during their residence. Ten have been masters for periods between fifteen and thirty years. The terms of ten masters have reached nearly fifteen years. Eight masters have been connected with the school between five and ten years. The periods of the remaining fifty-one have varied from two to five years.

It is interesting to notice that among the seventy-nine masters have been graduates of about twenty different Colleges. For example: Twelve have been graduates of Harvard, eleven of Trinity, three of Yale, four of Columbia,

---

1880. Augustus Muhlenberg Swift, was a master for ten years, from 1873 to 1883. He died of fever in Rome, Italy, March 27, 1884, and was interred in the English Burial Ground, where a beautiful monument marks the last resting place of his remains.

The Rev. Thomas G. Valpey was a master from 1860 to 1868. In 1868, receiving a pressing invitation from his old friend and college pastor, Bishop Littlejohn, to come to Brooklyn and start a school, he left St Paul's. But seven years later he returned to Concord, and from 1875 to the day of his death, November 15, 1890, he was connected with the school, being principally occupied in teaching Greek. Mr. Valpey, by general consent of those who know the results of his training, was very successful in imparting a sound knowledge of elementary Greek and in laying a stable foundation for good scholarship. His fidelity to every duty assigned him and his conscientious anxiety to make his pupils do well were very marked traits of his character. Nor was he wanting in affectionate regard for the boys and all his friends. No master was at heart more solicitous for the real good of the school and no one was more ready to take pains for its welfare.

three of Hobart, three of Brown, one of Dartmouth, two of Oxford (England), three of Cambridge (England), one of Williams, one of Johns Hopkins, one of University of Pennsylvania, one of Rutgers, and so on. Twenty-eight masters have been alumni of the school.

The Statement for the session 1889-'90 contained a list of twenty-seven masters besides the rector and vice-rector. The rector has been in office thirty-five years; the vice-rector twenty-five years. Three of the twenty-seven masters have resided at the school for more than twenty years, eight of them for more than ten years, and six for more than five years. Three were graduates of Yale, one of Harvard, two of Columbia, five of Trinity, one of Oxford, one of Brown, one of Hobart, one of Rutgers, and so on. These facts show that the school has been able to retain through a long series of years the services of competent men. One of the great difficulties in carrying on a school such as St. Paul's is to get capable masters. Mere knowledge and ability to teach are not sufficient qualifications. There must be besides, high principle, good manners, much tact, patience, and hopefulness. To be really happy in dealing and living with boys a variety of qualities and accomplishments is necessary. A dull man is always a failure; a man who can neither laugh merrily himself nor make others laugh is not usually successful as a master. Nor can a nervous and sensitive man ever find the life a pleasant one. A power to discriminate between trivial annoying faults and grave defects of character is absolutely essential. Self-control, ability to restrain tongue and temper, courage, generosity, manliness, are all needed in one who lives with boys and would gain their confidence and respect. Moreover, where a company of thirty men with different temperaments and diverse training and experience live together, engaged in a common work, the success of their efforts and the good of the whole body can only be secured by an honorable regard for each other, by patient toleration of the inevitable peculiarities of individuals, and by a cordial recognition of the fact that in such a life one has no right to expect his own judgment or opinion always to prevail. A critical, carping master, who constantly finds fault either with his associates, or with the regulations and decisions by which the school is governed, only injures where he ought to help, and aggravates the difficulties of those who have the chief responsibility. In England there is always a large number of men who have passed through the public schools and universities and are highly educated in mind and body, and who also possess many of the aptitudes essential to the successful master. They have themselves seen how able and good men win the affection and trust of boys and train them to become fine manly fellows. The best examples have been set them, and they have but to follow in clearly-marked paths in order to succeed as teachers. But in this country there have been no great boarding schools, such as Eton and Harrow, and of late years, when places like St. Paul's have been founded, the men who conduct them have been obliged to form their methods by their own judgment and observation, and to learn their business from daily experience.

St. Paul's has been highly favored in its staff of instructors. The spirit of anxious desire for the welfare of the boys, of untiring work in their behalf, of kindly judgment and patience in dealing with them, and of thoughtful prevision for their happiness, which has characterized the head of the school has in various degrees characterized the whole body of masters. As one of the oldest and most valued of the instructors said not long ago: "It is Dr. Coit's large and generous way of treating men and boys, and the confidence inspired by his high and upright character, which have kept masters devoted to St. Paul's for long terms of years, and have constantly induced alumni to return to the school, as to a home, all the recollections of which are delightful." A great deal of a master's work is laborious and trying. There are many petty yet important details which need the experienced oversight of the older men. There is a large class of duties which, always irksome, become more so as years go on. Steadfast principle and a genuine care for the boys are required to keep a man as vigilant about small matters relating to health and manners, as he is about good lessons, and proper behavior in class room and study. Neither the salaries nor the accommodations of masters have been in past years all that could be desired, although the arrangements have been the best which the school's finances and buildings admitted. But in each new house better and more suitable quarters have been provided for the masters; the seven with families now occupy well-built and comfortable cottages.

It is right to say that the men engaged in the work have been painstaking, self-sacrificing, and zealous from no selfish motives, and from no seeking for gain or personal ease. They have been animated by a genuine pride in the place, by a sincere desire to advance its welfare and to further the plans of the rector. They have been singularly free from jealousies and quarrels, and they have joined cordially and generously in all the various enterprises for the improvement of the school. Many of them well deserve to be accounted among its true benefactors.

If any one were asked what are the distinguishing characteristics of the discipline and government of St. Paul's, it would be hard to give an answer which would convey an exact account. There are several quite different sorts of government existing in boarding schools. One may be called the free system, under which very little restraint or supervision is exercised; which is only strict in regard to lessons and certain outward aspects of conduct, but does not aim at formation of character. Another is the military plan, where the life and regulations of the barrack are imitated, and the soldier is the type which is cultivated after a fashion. Another, happily not very common, is what may be termed the espionage method, under which boys are watched with the specific purpose of finding out what they say and do, where they are neither trusted nor readily believed, and under which there is always an exaggeration of their faults. There is also the parental system, in which the attempt is made to reproduce the features of a good home and to deal with the scholars as a wise father deals with his sons. In behalf of all these ways of governing a community of boys, except that in which espionage is used, much may be said. And this moreover is certain, that each one of these methods, with the exception already made. furnishes great advantages in the training and development of certain classes of boys. If it were possible to combine harmoniously the best features of the free, the military, and the parental forms of government, a system could be framed which would probably comprehend a larger number of individuals with happier results than any other.

The end aimed at in any rational scheme of education is the formation of good character, both mental and moral, with healthy bodies; and character is based on habits. The studies pursued, the methods of teaching, the customs and regulations adopted, are chiefly valuable in so far as they tend to produce certain habits. It is quite true that Cæsar's Commentaries, the Æneid, the Iliad, Anabasis, are great works of literature; that the processes of elementary algebra and the truths of geometry are necessary for the prosecution of certain scientific studies. But their real worth in the discipline of a boy's mind does not depend simply upon intrinsic merit. The reason why the classics are so largely employed in education is because they are instruments which when handled by competent instructors have power to form such habits as attention, intelligent observation, and clear expression of thought. They have been found most useful in enlarging a boy's vocabulary, in cultivating his memory, in giving exercise to his judgment and other faculties, and in forming a taste for literature. A large part of what a boy learns at school quickly fades from his recollection and apparently is entirely useless to him in after life. But the mental habits which he acquires through the use of his faculties, in learning and reciting his lessons, prove of the highest and most enduring value if he is taught in the right way. Good teaching therefore is teaching which forms and cultivates good mental habits. In like manner the discipline and regulations of a school ought to aim chiefly at the production and nurture of certain practical virtues. Truthfulness, fidelity to trusts, honesty, obedience, courage, generosity, respect for sacred places and things, loyalty to home and friends, self-restraint, straightforwardness, punctuality, neatness, cleanness in word and deed, love of country, and a genuine fear of God; these are the qualities which a schoolmaster who has the true welfare of boys at heart desires to see growing up in them as the results of the influence and discipline under which they live. These are the results sought to be attained at St. Paul's, and all the regulations, customs, and arrangements are designed for their furtherance. The rector and his assistants perceive more clearly and with keener regret than other persons how far short of its high ideal the school falls. The histories of nearly all such establishments as that at Concord contain the record of various mistakes and failures, and St. Paul's makes no claim to be an exception. But every Concordian will cordially grant that the *aim* of the discipline, teaching, and training of the school has been to make boys honorable gentlemen, good citizens and Christians. At first the system of government was modelled as closely as possible after that of a Christian home. As long as there was only a small number of boys, it was possible for the rector to exercise a very direct personal influence over every one of them, to know each one thoroughly, and to watch over the training and development of character in each with the same sort of attentive interest and affection as is exercised in a well-ordered home. But with the growth of the school came necessarily various changes. What was feasible with a few was out of the question with many. More systematic discipline had to be introduced than was needed at first. Certain rules and customs were now prescribed; certain offenses had to be defined and their penalties attached. The rector's direct contact with each member of the school became less, and hence means had to be devised through which he could know the different individuals of his charge and by which his influence could be exerted on all. This is the reason why the reports for all violations of order and for neglects of every sort have always been made to him, and why he has retained for himself the reception of excuses and the allotment of penalties. For the same reason all permissions conferring privileges must come from him, and all changes of the work of a boy, and any special arrangements for his instruction are referred to him. In the Thursday evening talk, or Lecture as it is called, the rector speaks directly to the boys on various topics connected with their daily life which could not be properly treated in the pulpit. The confirmation class, meeting once a week during several months of the session, affords another opportunity for his direct personal intercourse with many of the pupils. The officers of the various clubs and societies consult with him in regard to all plans for the improvement of these bodies. The arrangements for the athletic sports, for the boating, for the cricket contests, for the Easter exhibition and dance, for the anniversary exercises, are all submitted to him, very often suggested by him. But these instances are only examples of the many and varied ways in which the rector of the school comes into direct and intimate relations with the boys, by which he gets to know them, and they come to know him. Through such means as these, although the number of scholars is now three hundred, it is possible for the head master to know every boy and to form beneficial ties and relations with each one. Of course his position as pastor of the entire community opens to him many other ways of reaching the hearts and consciences of his flock. That the office is a most laborious one, involving grave responsibilities and multifarious duties, is evident from the nature of the case. Besides a large and exacting correspondence, there devolves upon him the oversight of the instruction, health, morals, and manners of three hundred boys, and the general care of a great estate. The selection of masters and the maintenance of cordial relations with a body of twenty-five men are no trifling parts of his office. In fact so numerous and arduous are the duties which he must necessarily discharge that only a man of vigorous constitution and large mental powers can hope to fulfil them with any fair measure of success.

As has already been intimated, the customs and regulations for the government of St. Paul's involve features belonging to the free, the military, and the home system. Punctuality, obedience, respectful behavior to masters and elders, and reverent conduct in chapel are enforced by influence, by wholesome traditions, and by such penalties as may be necessary. But the effort is constantly made to induce boys to practice these virtues, as well as such vital ones as truthfulness, honesty, and the like, from right feeling, from genuine principle, and not simply under the pressure of rules and punishments. The number of special rules concerning order and conduct, in addition to those prescribed at all times and places by good manners and common sense, is very small. The school is governed chiefly by an unwritten code of customs and traditions which do not need to be printed or often rehearsed. A fair-minded boy with the instincts and feelings of a gentleman understands very soon the spirit of the place, what is expected from him, what he may do and not do. The temptation in all boarding schools is to overdo or underdo the care and watchfulness expended upon the boys. If there is too much supervision, too much restraint, a boy's character suffers; there must be room left for his tastes and dispositions to display themselves naturally and for the exercise, to some extent, of his own choice and judgment as to conduct. Too much repression tends to make hypocrites or to produce moral weakness instead of moral strength. Too much freedom and too little guidance during the years when character is forming are apt to make passions and appetites unruly and to give headway to self-will. Undoubtedly there is a great deal of supervision at St. Paul's, but there is also much freedom. There are many times and many respects in which the individual's conduct is left to be determined by his own sense of propriety, his own decisions as to what is right or wrong, honorable or dishonorable. No such impossible state is hoped for as an entire absence of selfish, reckless, idle, and poorly disposed boys. They are quantities which can not be eliminated from any large school. What is sought to be done by the supervision and restraint at St. Paul's is to give vantage and help to the good traits in every boy, to encourage and protect the weak or wavering characters, and, as far as possible, to prevent evil tendencies from becoming the prevailing ones. A large part of the supervision has the health of the boys for its object; much of it is natural—that is, it comes from the fact that boys and masters live together in the same households and are brought in contact by the mere routine of daily life and without set purpose. Where the masters are experienced men, themselves manly and straightforward, with genuine liking and regard for the boys, this intercourse is most beneficial; and the fact that as a rule the relations between boys and masters are really cordial and kindly and that the alumni cherish warm and affectionate regard for their former teachers is the best proof that there is no suspicious surveillance practiced at the school, and no such restraint as interferes with a scholar's self-respect.

As to the religious customs of the place, the daily prayers, the observance of Sunday, and the direct influences employed to lead a boy to confirmation and holy communion, there has often been criticism; but the criticism is in many cases based on exaggerated or distorted accounts of what actually takes place. The following are the facts:

The whole household attends prayers in the chapel every morning. The service consists of a hymn, a psalm from the Psalter, the Apostles' Creed, and suitable collects. It lasts scarcely fifteen minutes. In the evening, directly after tea, there is a short service in each house, occupying about five minutes; a hymn is sung and a few prayers said. Just before the studies are dismissed for the day an interval of five minutes is set apart for Bible reading. The older boys who are out of the study are left entirely free as to this matter. Of course, as far as personal influence can affect them, they are urged to form the habit of reading the Bible daily. On Sunday three services are obligatory. At nine o'clock the shortened form of morning prayer is said, and occupies about thirty minutes. The second service is held at 11.30 A. M., and consists of the communion office with sermon. The boys leave after the prayer for Christ's Church Militant. They are rarely in chapel more than an hour at this service. The shortened form of evening prayer, with sermon, is used in the afternoon at 3.15, and takes ordinarily three quarters of an hour. The entire time devoted to the chapel services on

Sunday is, on an average, not quite two hours and a half, which does not seem an excessive amount. The division of the morning service into two parts is a custom first introduced at St. Paul's, College Point, by Dr. Muhlenberg, with the object of making that service less tiring to boys. For the same reason the custom has prevailed at Concord. Every pains is taken to have the services bright and hearty, and not too long. The ritual in use is simple, but it is meant to be reverent and dignified—to edify the congregation and not to furnish a spectacle. A short sacred lesson is recited in the afternoon by all the members of the school below the fifth form. At 8.30 P. M. the whole school assembles in the "Big Study," a translation of the ancient Latin hymn *Grates peracto jam die* is sung, the old Mosaic benediction is given, and a general hand-shaking and exchange of good-night take place. Undoubtedly the day is well filled up, but is it too full? There is a large space of time left for walks, letter-writing, visiting, and reading. Not more than an hour is spent in the study and only a half-hour in recitation. The day would be tedious if there were not plenty of occupations to fill up its hours; and a good test of the reasonable character of its arrangements may be found in the fact that it is not remembered as irksome or disagreeable by the great majority of those who have left the school. It is true that many of the boys spend Sunday quite differently at home; but it may be asked whether their home way of spending Sunday is always the best way, tending to help them to grow up good Christian men. The difficulty of making the school Sunday an innocent, happy, and sacred day, and the danger of pressing too many religious observances on the boys are recognized, but the results of nearly thirty years seem to justify the retention of the present order. The boys frequently have the opportunity of hearing very distinguished preachers. Not a term goes by now in which able and edifying sermons by eminent clergymen are not delivered. In a four-years' residence at St. Paul's a boy will hear many of the best preachers in America.

The roll of the alumni, published in the spring of 1890, and the list of scholars in the last Statement, give together 1,872 names. Of this whole number of boys who have attended St. Paul's School during the thirty-four years of its existence, about one hundred and fifty have either been on scholarships, or have received a total remission of the annual charges for tuition and residence, or have had large reductions from those charges granted to them. The actual deduction from the school income due to these grants has exceeded fifty thousand dollars. The boys to whom these favors have been extended have in nearly all cases proved worthy of them. The alumni and other friends of St. Paul's may take just pride in the honorable fact that the rector has devoted to the support and assistance of deserving scholars, in the form of remissions and reductions, a sum of money which is equal to twenty per cent at least of all the profits due to the strict economy that has been practised.

The years must inevitably bring great changes at St. Paul's. Much has been done, but much remains to be done before the school will possess that assured position and complete equipment which it must have for permanence and for maintaining the reputation it has gained. What it is now is chiefly the result of the self-sacrificing labors of the rector, and of the combined and devoted efforts of men who have given to it their best years and powers. The preceding pages show what a large assemblage of admirable apparatus and influences for the work of education already exists. Whatever errors of judgment may have characterized methods of instruction, religious training, or discipline in the past, the main features of the plan on which the school is conducted have been proved to be sound and judicious. In illustration of this one need only adduce the devotion of the alumni, the cordial and warm support given by parents from all quarters of the United States, and the approval of experienced men of the world as well as that of earnest Churchmen.

Americans give generously and nobly to objects which they think will benefit their country or the Church. They have been particularly liberal to universities and colleges. St. Paul's, although but a school, has found warm friends to whom she is deeply indebted. She still needs their help to bring to completion the work which has so far advanced. Perhaps this account will show that she is worthy of the support and help she seeks, and that to endow her with scholarships and with funds sufficient to maintain her work and to protect her against adversity are objects which may justly claim the benevolent regard of true lovers of Church and country.

This sketch of St. Paul's School is laudatory of many features of the work and of many persons who have had part in it. The readers of the foregoing pages must pardon the natural bias of one, who having shared in the toils, anxieties, and disappointments of the past, delights to record, perhaps, with too partial regard, what has been hitherto accomplished, and to indulge in fond hopes of future enlargement and prosperity. The writer has had in view, not the general public, for whom this account would have little or no interest, but the alumni and their friends, and those few persons who are specially interested in schools for boys.

But no mere material improvement or progress, no praise of even the most warm-hearted friends, can furnish the true grounds for satisfaction, or crown the labor with its best rewards. The value of the education at St. Paul's must be measured by its influence on those who go out into the world bearing the impress of the training and associations they have had at the school. Those boys who pass through college without stain, who practice amid varied scenes of temptation, self-restraint, genuine love of parents and kindred, fidelity to duties and trusts, and honest use of opportunities, add more to the good repute of St. Paul's than any words of praise from others can add, and give more sincere pleasure to their old masters and friends than the most liberal benefactions for special needs and objects can convey. "Surrexerunt filii ejus, et beatissimam prædicaverunt," was the Wise Man's praise of the good mother. In a certain true sense the words may be applied to any school for boys the chief aim of which is to give sound training in morals, manners, and learning. May St. Paul's ever prove worthy of such precious beatitude! May many be found to-day and in future generations rising up to invoke blessings on their old school for the good they have received within its walls! It is on the conduct and success of those who go from St. Paul's to the great colleges, or into business, and pass to their places in social and national life that the reputation, the prosperity, and the growth of the school will depend.

THE END.

BIBLIOLIFE

Old Books Deserve a New Life
www.bibliolife.com

Did you know that you can get most of our titles in our trademark **EasyScript**[TM] print format? **EasyScript**[TM] provides readers with a larger than average typeface, for a reading experience that's easier on the eyes.

Did you know that we have an ever-growing collection of books in many languages?

Order online:
www.bibliolife.com/store

Or to exclusively browse our **EasyScript**[TM] collection:
www.bibliogrande.com

At BiblioLife, we aim to make knowledge more accessible by making thousands of titles available to you – quickly and affordably.

Contact us:
BiblioLife
PO Box 21206
Charleston, SC 29413